Schizophrenia Revealed

Also by Michael Foster Green

Schizophrenia from a Neurocognitive Perspective:
Probing the Impenetrable Darkness

A NORTON PROFESSIONAL BOOK

Schizophrenia Revealed

From Neurons to Social Interactions

Michael Foster Green, Ph.D.

W·W·NORTON

NEW YORK · LONDON

Photograph, page 39: Copyright 1971. From *Exceptional Infant: Studies in Abnormality* by M.F. Waldrop and C. F. Halverson. Reproduced by permission of Taylor & Francis, Inc., http://www.routledge-ny.com.

Illustration, page 40: From *Second-trimester markers of fetal size in schizophrenia: A study of monozygotic twins.* Volume 149, 1355–1361, 1992. Copyright 1992, the American Psychiatric Association. Reprinted by permission.

Illustration, page 67: Reprinted by permission of Elsevier Science from "Alternative Phenotypes for the Complex Genetics of Schizophrenia," by R. Freedman, L. E. Adler, and S. Leonard. *Biological Psychiatry,* vol. 45, 551–558. Copyright 1999 by the Society of Biological Psychiatry.

Figure 5 of color insert: From O'Leary et al., Auditory attentional deficits in patients with schizophrenia. A PET study. *Archives of General Psychiatry, 53,* 1996: 633–641. Courtesy of the American Medical Association.

Photograph, figure 7 of color insert: From *Hydrotherapy in Psychiatric Hospitals* by Rebekah Wright. Boston, MA: The Tudor Press, 1940.

Copyright © 2003, 2001 by Michael Foster Green

For information about permission to reproduce
selections from this book, write to
Permissions, W. W. Norton & Company, Inc.,
500 Fifth Avenue, New York, NY 10110

Composition and book design by Ecomlinks, Inc.
Manufacturing by Haddon Craftsmen
Production Manager: Leeann Graham

Library of Congress Cataloging-in-Publication Data
Green, Michael Foster.
  Schizophrenia revealed: from neurons to social interactions/ Michael Foster Green.
    p. cm.—(A Norton professional book)
  Includes bibliographical references and index.
  ISBN 0-393-70334-7
  1. Schizophrenia. I. Title II. Series.

RC514.G694 2001
616.89'82—dc21   2001018041

ISBN 0-393-70418-1 (pbk)

W. W. Norton & Company, Inc., 500 Fifth Avenue, New York, NY 10110
www.wwnorton.com
W. W. Norton & Company, Ltd., 10 Coptic Street, London WC1A 1PU
  3 4 5 6 7 8 9 0

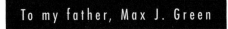
To my father, Max J. Green

Contents

For many years, schizophrenia was considered a deep and profound mystery. It was generally viewed as unknown and unknowable, beyond the reach of science, more like metaphysics than like a brain disease. This is no longer the case. Schizophrenia may still hold many puzzles and paradoxes, refusing to fit into any of our existing categories of disorders, but recent developments have made it more comprehensible. To make sense of schizophrenia, we need to approach it in a fresh way.

One reason that schizophrenia appeared mysterious for so long was because we failed to ask the right questions. Although the illness consists of a wide range of features, there has been an understandable temptation to concentrate on its more dramatic symptoms (such as hallucinations and delusions). This narrow focus caused us to miss important aspects of treatment and outcome. Until recently, there was more emphasis on psychotic symptoms than on neurocognitive deficits, more emphasis on illness onset than on the premorbid period, more emphasis on reducing symptoms than on reducing disability, more emphasis on rehospitalization rates than on community re-entry. But major developments in scientific research during the 1990s have changed the way we look at the illness. A new view of schizophrenia is emerging from clinical research and neuroscience, and the view is radically different from the previous one. It ties together astute observations from the beginning of the twentieth century with impressive technological developments from the end of the century.

Schizophrenia Revealed reviews the key developments in schizophrenia research during the last decade. Every effort has been made to convey the excitement and importance of these scientific advances and to make them accessible to the general reader. No previous courses in psychology are required, only a curiosity about schizophrenia. We begin with descriptions of the features of the illness, and then summarize our current understanding of how the nervous system develops in schizophrenia. Next we explain how problems in brain development can lead to neurocognitive deficits. We then discuss what genetic and brain imaging techniques have taught us about schizophrenia. The last two chapters of the book cover the clinically relevant topics of intervention and outcome.

Over the course of the following chapters, schizophrenia will become more comprehensible, less mysterious, but no less compelling. As a disease, it is humbling and enigmatic, timeless and global. The origins of the disease are present at birth, but the illness plays out over decades. It extracts a devastating toll on the individual, the family, and society. Schizophrenia defies expectations and ignores intuition. Among all the maladies and disorders that challenge our species, there is, quite simply, nothing else like it.

Preface to the Paperback Edition

In the years since *Schizophrenia Revealed* was first published, the field of study has experienced rapid changes. For a field that has tended to change rather slowly over time, developments have been occurring at a dizzying rate. This progress, for the most part, reinforces the appropriateness of my earlier decisions about the content and direction of the book.

I have no regrets about building the book on the "three pillars" of schizophrenia: disrupted neural connections, neurocognitive deficits, and functional impairment. This structure still strikes me as valid. Yet as it was my intention to write a relatively short and readable book, I am keenly aware that some potentially important material was left out.

A few of the impressive advances of the past few years are worth mentioning now, as the paperback edition is being published. These are limited to two areas of the book: genetics (Chapter 3) and interventions (Chapter 6).

The chapter on genetics refers to two areas of promise for the future. I did not expect the future to arrive so soon. First, genetic association studies are starting bear fruit. These are highly focused genetic studies that start with the selection of a particular gene, one that is considered relevant to the disorder. This approach requires scientists to know the role of a candidate gene (i.e., what protein it creates), as well as to have a very good hunch about the role of this protein in schizophrenia. Because dopamine has long been associated with schizophrenia, it comes as no surprise that a gene involved with the metabolism of dopamine has become one target for genetic association studies. It turns out that the different versions of this gene (i.e., its alleles) account for some of the differences in cognitive performance in patients. In other words, patients with some alleles have better performance on average than patients with others. This is one of the first pieces of evidence for a direct link from gene to cognitive deficit in schizophrenia.

Another development in the genetics of schizophrenia is the increasing focus on the use of alternative phenotypes. The basic paradox is that, for the genetics of schizophrenia to make real progress, studies will probably need to use a phenotype other than schizophrenia. The problem stems from the fact someone with schizophrenia-relevant genes, may, or may not, have schizophrenia. Alternative phenotypes are believed to be much closer to the schizophrenia-relevant genes and should be detectable, even in people who do not have the disorder. In the last couple of years, large-scale studies of schizophrenia have been initiated that use an alternative phenotype, such as a cognitive performance measure, or a response on an electrophysiological test. These studies will direct the study of the genetics of schizophrenia from the consideration of conventional phenotypes of a clinical diagnosis to the much more promising task of identifying genes tied to risk factors for schizophrenia.

In the area of interventions, families and patients will be heartened to learn that a new drug was recently approved in the United States for the treatment of schizophrenia. Abilify (aripiprazole) works by means of a very different mechanism of action than other antipsychotic medications. All other antipsychotic medications act as blockers (antagonists) at the dopamine receptor. Abilify is a partial agonist at the dopamine receptor, meaning that, instead of blocking receptor activity, it creates slow and steady activity at the receptor. By analogy, one can think of this pharmacological quality in terms of the difference between a drug that keeps a door shut (antagonist) and one that jams the door just a little open (partial agonist). The benefit for schizophrenic patients is that side effects that stem from having the door completely closed are mild with Abilify.

Lastly, the treatment of neurocognitive deficits in schizophrenia is receiving deserved attention and is no longer a mere scientific curiosity. The importance of these deficits for the daily functioning of patients is now widely recognized. Also, there is optimism about new types of drugs that might be effective for improving cognition in schizophrenia. In a new initiative sponsored by the U.S. National Institute of Mental Health and awarded to UCLA, a series of consensus meeting will be held over the next two years to develop standards, guidelines, and procedures in this area. The presence of standards will encourage scientists in the pharmaceutical industry to develop and test drugs for treating neurocognitive deficits in schizophrenia. Essentially, the goal of these consensus meetings will be to map out a pathway by which the considerable resources of the pharmaceutical industry can be directed into this area. If successful, this initiative will allow patients to enjoy enriched lives.

Although the field is advancing fast, the conclusions of the book have not changed. Schizophrenia is still, I would argue, the world's most enigmatic disorder. The one thing that has changed is that more people now know about schizophrenia. Two years ago I never would have imagined that the Academy Award for best picture of 2001 would go to a movie about schizophrenia (*A Beautiful Mind*). Although the movie may not have been a faithful recreation of the life of its protagonist, John Forbes Nash, it provided a largely accurate depiction of the disorder and succeeded in giving a human dimension to an impersonal disease.

These are times that warrant optimism despite the fundamental seriousness of this disease. The science of schizophrenia has typically moved slower than other areas of neuroscience. Not anymore. New approaches, new ideas, and new treatments, all lead to the conviction that, by moving beyond old ways of thinking, we can expect better days.

Michael F. Green
February 2003

Acknowledgments

In this book I tried to capture the exciting developments that have occurred in schizophrenia research during the past decade. Many of the ideas expressed here stem from long discussions over the years with my outstanding colleagues at the UCLA Department of Psychiatry and Biobehavioral Sciences and at the Department of Veterans Affairs, VISN 22, Mental Illness Research Education and Clinical Center. In particular, Keith Nuechterlein, Ph.D.; John Brekke, Ph.D.; and Joel Braslow, M.D., Ph.D., served as excellent resources for sections of this book. Researchers from other institutions, including Nancy Andreasen, M.D., Ph.D.; Monte Buchsbaum, M.D.; Shatij Kapur, M.D., Ph.D.; Alexander Stevens, Ph.D.; and Elaine Walker, Ph.D. took time out of their hectic schedules to provide me with photos and brain scans.

Mary Jane Robertson, M.S., gave detailed and thoughtful feedback on every draft of the manuscript. As someone who has both strong writing skills and a good general knowledge of the topics, she established a flow and continuity for the text that would have been missing otherwise. I wish to thank the staff at W.W. Norton who have been wonderfully helpful since the start of this endeavor. Special thanks goes to my editor, Deborah Malmud, who used a seemingly endless supply of colored pencils to greatly improve the quality and readability of the book.

Above all, I wish to thank my wife, Eva, and our daughter, Lora, who initially encouraged me to write this book and then tolerated the frequent absences from the dinner table that came as a result. Without them, this book would not have been written.

Schizophrenia Revealed

Chapter One

Features
of Schizophrenia

There are no secrets.
There is no mystery.
There is only common sense.
Saying attributed to the Onondaga Indians

Demystifying the Mysterious Illness

Schizophrenia is shrouded in an overpowering sense of mystery—which is a wonderful quality for a romance or a novel but not for an illness. When an illness is viewed as inexplicable and impenetrable, people tend to react to it with one of two extremes: either they *stigmatize* the illness or they *romanticize* it. It's hard to know which is worse. Both reactions are readily observable today, but they were especially pronounced during the second half of the 1960s, a pivotal period for mental health in general, and for schizophrenia in particular.

The 1960s witnessed a historic trend for mental health: the exodus of psychotic patients out of the remote state hospitals into the community. If this sounds familiar, it is because a similar exodus occurred during the 1990s when states not only decided to close hospitals but agencies also decided to limit lengths of stay (thereby swelling the ranks of the homeless). In contrast to the recent exodus, which was driven by finances, the exodus in the 1960s was driven by ideology. For reasons that were more optimistic than rational, many believed that psychotic patients would improve if treated in the community.

The exodus from state hospitals began in the late 1950s and gained momentum during the second half of the 1960s. It was accelerated both by the 1963 Community Mental Health Centers Act (signed into law a month before President Kennedy was assassinated) and the introduction in 1965 of Medicaid and Medicare. By the late 1960s, hundreds of thousands of psychotic patients who might otherwise have been out of sight were living in the community. As a result, many people in the community who had never previously encountered psychotic patients before, were now coming into direct contact with them. The result was predictable—the general population was mystified by severely ill patients and reacted with fear and distrust.

The 1960s was also famous for an "anti-psychiatry" movement. This movement still exists today, but its influence is negligible. The original proponents of this movement claimed that psychosis (including schizophrenia) was a "myth"—a creation of society, not biology. They viewed mental illness more as an adjustment problem or a difficulty in living than as a brain disorder. Medications and hospitalization, they argued, were not needed to treat psychosis; not only were they unnecessary, but medications in particular might interfere with one's self-healing. Psychosis became a journey of self-discovery, a deep and profound growth process, or even a rational response to an insane world. Schizophrenia became romanticized.

One way to assess the underlying feelings of a culture is to consider the popular cult films of that time. In 1966, when patients were rapidly leaving long-term hospitals for the community, two movies captured antithetical views of mental illness. The films do not specifically refer to schizophrenia, but they clearly involve chronic psychotic patients, most of whom would have schizophrenia by modern criteria. The movies are remarkable, both in terms of their similarities and their differences. The films were released the same year and were both set in France. Each received critical acclaim and became highly popular cult films on college campuses. One film starred a famous British actor, the other launched the career of a now-famous British actress. Both movies explored the same question, namely, what happens when chronically institutionalized psychotic inpatients have their institutional constraints removed?

The King of Hearts, set during the last part of World War I, is the story of a Scottish soldier (played by Alan Bates) who is sent to scout out a quaint French town that has recently been under German occupation. The town is abandoned by the troops, but not before they hide some bombs and set them to explode in the town square the following day (when British troops are expected to take over the village). The French residents learn of the plan and flee, leaving the town empty except for inmates from the local insane asylum. The patients soon emerge from the asylum only to find a deserted town: they help themselves to colorful costumes and assume the roles of local town characters. The patients have a charming childlike naïveté and manage well on their own. By the time Bates arrives, the patients have made their town so congenial that it takes him a long time to realize these people are psychotic. When he finally figures out that the town is about to explode, Bates readies the patients for evacuation. But they cannot comprehend the unseen—explosives hidden inside their town walls—even though they are well aware of the explosions outside of their town walls. As a result, the psychotic patients are afraid to leave. After unsuccessfully trying to convince them of the hidden danger, Bates loses his temper, forcefully reminding one of them that "Yesterday, you were in a nut house!" The man wonders aloud if Bates is jealous and just as forcefully reminds him that "Yesterday, you were outside with 'the others.'" The psychiatric patients had created an endearing community that seemed like an island of sanity compared with the horrors of war raging just outside the town gates.

The other popular cult film, *Marat Sade,* presents a starkly different picture of severe mental illness. It is a dark and edgy view of institutional life. This movie is cleverly structured: It is both a play within a play and a telling of one historical event within another. Toward the end of his life, the marquis de Sade (of sadism fame) was incarcerated in the Charenton asylum in France. The movie is set in 1808 in the asylum; de Sade is writing a play about the assassination of Jean-Paul Marat, a leader of the French Revolution who was stabbed in his bathtub by Charlotte Corday (played by Glenda Jackson). The marquis writes and directs the play during his incarceration, using the psychotic patients as actors. The performance is for the enjoyment of the warden's family and friends. Much of the dialogue involves themes of liberty from the French Revolution. During the performance, the patients become increasingly infected with a revolutionary fervor, and the action escalates into such an uncontrolled and violent riot that they start attacking the audience.

Consider the messages of the two films. The romantic view of *The King of Hearts* implies that psychotic inpatients are sensitive souls who have trouble tolerating the crazy world around them. They would manage fine if only left alone. The stigmatizing view of *Marat Sade* implies that mental illness strips away the inhibitions that are necessary to restrain our base and destructive impulses.

Schizophrenia will be romanticized and stigmatized as long as it remains a mysterious illness. It need not remain so. Although we do not yet have an adequate understanding of schizophrenia, an explosion of new scientific findings over the last decade has rendered the disorder much more comprehensible. But there is a catch: To make sense of the disorder, we need to think "outside the box" and to adopt a new focus. Efforts to clarify schizophrenia will backfire if we manage to get the facts right but still get the focus wrong.

Consider one of the most common misconceptions about schizophrenia—that it involves multiple personalities. This mistaken view is widespread and unfortunately reinforced by the media. A recent promotion for a nationally televised special on schizophrenia shamelessly beckoned viewers to go "inside the multiple minds of schizophrenics." Schizophrenia, however, is unrelated to multiple personalities; it is instead a distinct disorder characterized by psychotic symptoms that include auditory hallucinations (hearing voices that no one else can hear) and delusions (for example, believing that your life is controlled by aliens from another planet, or that the CIA is poisoning your food). These symptoms are *not* consistent with multiple personality disorder. As experts in mental health issues, we proudly correct this basic misunderstanding about schizophrenia wherever we can (in the classroom, the clinic, on long flights, and at dinner parties). But we may be making matters worse. In essence we are converting the *uneducated* lay person, who thinks that schizophrenia is multiple personalities, into the *educated* lay person, who now thinks that schizophrenia is like living in a Wes Craven horror movie. By getting the facts right, but the focus wrong, we inadvertently transform an illness that was only partially mysterious into one that is completely mysterious.

Recent scientific developments have given us a better understanding of schizophrenia and made it less mysterious. This new view approaches the illness in a fundamentally different way. The key lies in accepting a paradoxical and counterintuitive principle that flies in the face of prevailing notions: that schizophrenia is a psychotic disorder, not primarily a disorder of psychotic symptoms. Instead, schizophrenia can be viewed as a disorder that starts with problems in establishing connections between neurons. The problems in neural connections lead to neurocognitive deficits including problems in the areas of attention, memory, perception, and problem solving. These neurocognitive deficits lead to misinterpretations and confusion, and ultimately to functional impairment (that is, problems in everyday living). The psychotic symptoms are part of the illness, but they are not central to it. As described by Ming Tsuang and colleagues, "psychosis is the 'fever' of severe mental illness—a serious, but nonspecific indicator" (Tsuang, Stone, & Faraone, 2000). When understood in this fashion, schizophrenia is unlikely to be romanticized or stigmatized—there will be little temptation to elevate or denigrate an illness of neural connections and neurocognitive deficits. That is, in fact, what happened with epilepsy.

Different Reactions to Two Disorders

Epilepsy, once considered a mysterious illness, no longer carries the baggage it once did, although the illness is still not adequately understood. But when epilepsy was seen as mysterious, reactions were entirely predictable: The illness was stigmatized and romanticized.

Stigmatization of epilepsy can be traced back at least to the New Testament (Porter, 1995). In the book of Luke, when Christ healed a child with convulsions, he was seen as casting out a demon. During much of European history, epilepsy was considered a punishment from God, or a curse from the devil. Supernatural causes of epilepsy were not limited to Christian Europe. In the Ottoman Empire, some thought seizures indicated an illicit sexual affair—a jealous spirit grabbed a rival by the throat and choked that person into unconsciousness. In Hindu mythology, there was a demon whose special role was to cause convulsions. Even after it was no longer attributed to supernatural forces, epilepsy was still stigmatized. Until the 1800s, individuals with epilepsy, or "falling sickness" as it was known, were housed with psychotic patients in asylums. When efforts were made to house the two types of patients separately, it was only because people feared that psychotic patients might "catch" epilepsy.

Simultaneously, there was a strong tendency to romanticize epilepsy. "A powerful tradition has purported to see affinities between epilepsy and greatness. In this view, epilepsy could be a 'sacred' disorder, one that even elevated the sufferer during the fit to godlike status." (Porter, 1995, p. 170). Many examples exist to support a perceived link between epilepsy and superhuman traits. Hercules was said to suffer from epilepsy. Suggestions abound that many great leaders, including Julius Caesar and Alexander the Great, were epileptic. The Russian author Dostoevski gave vivid descriptions of his auras before a seizure. The auras took on a spiritual and religious meaning for him; he thought that he was touching God and claimed to experience extreme happiness that healthy (non-epileptic) people cannot imagine.

What happened to demystify epilepsy, and can the same thing happen for schizophrenia? It probably helped that the neural basis of epilepsy was established early in the nineteenth century, whereas a specific brain abnormality in schizophrenia has remained elusive. If the identification of a neural basis for epilepsy supplanted the previous supernatural views and demystified the illness, then perhaps all we need to demystify schizophrenia is a firmer neural explanation. But schizophrenia will not give up its mystery so easily. For the most part, schizophrenia is already considered a brain disease—even by people who are not sure what it is—and this realization has not helped. The reason schizophrenia has remained mysterious even after it was viewed as a brain disease lies in a fundamental disconnection—the brain disorder has no obvious linkage to the psychotic symptoms.

Consider a prototypical TV news program on schizophrenia. It probably starts by interviewing a schizophrenic person who offers a gripping description of frequent auditory hallucinations and bizarre delusions. In the next scene, the same patient is seen lying in a doughnut-shaped object that takes up an entire room—it is the latest model brain scanner. The next scene shows intent doctors hovering over complex monitors, pushing buttons and adjusting dials. Finally, we see the resulting brain scan, which is spectacular in color and detail. Sure enough, some regions of the patient's brain are abnormal in size, or abnormal in activity level (depending on the type of brain scan used). That settles it: The viewer is sold on the idea that schizophrenia is a brain disease. Yet the disorder has become no more understandable and no less mysterious because the symptoms of the illness have no obvious link to the results of the brain scan.

In this chapter, we will describe the symptoms of schizophrenia. An understanding of symptoms is essential, even if schizophrenia is not primarily a disorder of psychotic symptoms. Symptoms are a focus of treatment, both pharmacological and behavioral. Most of the time, clinical symptoms are distressing to patients. They lead to unhappiness, erratic behavior, and sometimes to violence or suicide. When a patient enters an emergency room in an agitated psychotic state, the first task is to stabilize the patient, which usually means bringing the symptoms under control. Also, for historical reasons, symptoms form the basis of the diagnosis. Diagnostic criteria change at a glacial rate. So, despite repeated calls by clinicians to replace a symptom-based diagnostic scheme with features of the illness that are more reliable and stable (Tsuang et al., 2000), diagnostic criteria are unlikely to shift dramatically away from symptoms in the near future.

Let us clarify what schizophrenia is *not* before we clarify what it *is*. First, as we mentioned above, schizophrenia is not multiple personalities. Though the term schizophrenia derives from the Greek words schizo (split) and phrene (mind), it was intended to refer to a fragmentation of different mental properties. Second, schizophrenia is not a direct result of the stress and fast pace of modern life. Rates of schizophrenia have been fairly stable over time, and this same disorder probably has been with us for centuries. Outcomes may vary depending on local mental health resources and attitudes toward illness, but schizophrenia is found throughout the world, even in decidedly nonmodern countries. Third, schizophrenia is not just a matter of believing in UFOs, alien abduction, past lives, or similar ideas. As we will see, the threshold for a diagnosis of schizophrenia is intentionally set rather high, and a diagnosis of the illness is not given out lightly. Unusual beliefs such as those mentioned above are considered "magical," but are not by themselves diagnostic of schizophrenia. Besides, as any resident of Southern California knows, the beliefs are too common to be pathological. Fourth, schizophrenia is not just believing that someone is after you. We all know that governments sometimes spy on their own citizens, and that ideas of persecution are sometimes justified. Beyond this, many people love a good conspiracy theory—consider America's decades-long obsession with John F. Kennedy's assassination. Paranoid delusions represent a heightened form of general suspiciousness, but even paranoid delusions are not diagnostic by themselves. The key point is that schizophrenia requires a constellation of features, and the diagnosis is not given for only a symptom or two. In brief, schizophrenia is defined as a mixture of characteristic signs and symptoms (including hallucinations, delusions, social withdrawal, etc.) that have been present during a 1-month period. Signs of the disorder must persist for at least six months and functional impairment must be present. The diagnosis of schizophrenia is described in more detail at the end of this chapter.

Slightly less than 1 percent of the world's population has schiz-ophrenia. Although this is a statistically low rate, it is common enough to create a huge problem for society. Most people know somebody with schizophrenia or know a family with an affected member. (Whether the problem is identified as schizophrenia or something else is another matter.) Schizophrenia affects men and woman about equally, but men tend to get the illness earlier and worse. Onset for men is typically in late teens and early twenties. Women typically have onsets in mid to late twenties, but onsets in later decades are not uncommon. Higher rates of schizophrenia are associated with lower socioeconomic status. There are two general explanations for this association: On the one hand, the stresses of living in a lower socioeconomic household or commu-nity might increase one's risk for schizophrenia (called social causation). Alternatively, lower socioeconomic status could be the direct result of an illness such as schizophrenia that leads to poor functioning and lower social and economic success (called social selection). Recent studies suggest reduced socioeconomic status may be a causative factor for other disorders (such as depression and substance abuse), but it is probably the result, not the cause, of schizophrenia (Dohrewend et al., 1992).

Schizophrenia is a very severe disorder. Only about a third of the patients with schizophrenia have a good outcome; maybe up to a half if a liberal definition of good outcome is used. About a third will have a paid job, although most of the time these jobs are in sheltered, instead of competitive, settings. The disorder is not only distressing to the individual and immensely disruptive to the family, it is also one of the world's leading causes of disability. Schizophrenia is among the top five causes of disability for young adults (both men and women) in developed regions of the world—more disabling than heart disease, arthritis, drug use, and HIV (Murray & Lopez, 1996). The total financial costs of this disability, in terms of the cost of treatment and lost productivity over the lifetime, are enormous—the annual cost of schizophre-nia in the United States alone amounts to about half the gross domestic product of countries like Denmark or Norway. No matter how one looks at it, or which perspective one takes, schizophrenia is exceedingly severe.

Early Views

Modern views of schizophrenia go back to the early part of the twentieth century, in particular to the contributions of two exceptional individuals: Emil Kraepelin and Eugen Bleuler. Emil Kraepelin was a German psychiatrist who developed an influential classification of psychiatric disorders in the late nineteenth and early twentieth centuries (Kraepelin, 1971). According to Kraepelin's classification, there were two major types of psychotic disorders: dementia praecox and manic depression. Dementia praecox, which literally means early dementia, was the name for schizophrenia at the time. In Kraepelin's classification, a key difference between the two disorders was that the prognosis (the expected outcome) of manic depression was much better than that of dementia praecox.

It was the Swiss psychiatrist Eugen Bleuler who changed both the conception and the name of dementia praecox (Bleuler, 1950). He reasoned, quite correctly, that many patients do not deteriorate, therefore it was not correct to use a term that meant early dementia. Admitting that "it is really quite impossible to find a perfect name for a concept which is still developing and changing" (p. 8), he nonetheless gave it a shot. Bleuler selected the name schizophrenia because he considered the splitting (schizo) of different psychic functions (phrene) to be one of its most important features. He thought this term was "less apt to be misunderstood" (p. 8) than dementia praecox. Unfortunately, the disorder had the misfortune of going from a label that was pessimistic and incorrect to one that became confusing and misleading.

Bleuler made a critical and insightful distinction between *fundamental* and *accessory* symptoms of schizophrenia. Fundamental symptoms included affectivity (mood), ambivalence, and alterations in association. Disturbance in association (loose associations in thought and speech) was afforded a special status as the abnormality most closely linked to the disease process. These simple fundamental symptoms combined to form compound fundamental symptoms, including disturbances in attention. Conveniently, most of Bleuler's fundamental symptoms start with the letter "A," thereby providing a mnemonic for students. Accessory symptoms, which were derived from the fundamental symptoms, included hallucinations, delusions, and a variety of behavioral and speech abnormalities. Although the symptoms were considered secondary in a causal sense, they were (and still are) important for treatment. As Bleuler wrote:

> It is not often that the fundamental symptoms are so markedly exhibited as to cause the patient to be hospitalized in a mental institution. It is primarily the accessory phenomena which make his retention at home impossible, or it is they which make the psychosis manifest and give occasion to require psychiatric help. These accessory symptoms may be present throughout the whole course of the disease, or only in entirely arbitrary periods of illness. (1950, p. 94)

Bleuler's insight was striking and counterintuitive—so counterintuitive that even historical accounts sometimes fail to appreciate it. In a recent book on the history of psychiatry, the author noted that: "Bleuler's distinction [between fundamental and accessory symptoms] looks particularly misconceived to our hindsight" (Hoenig, 1995, p. 343). On the contrary, if we jettison incorrect assumptions, Bleuler's distinction looks particularly well conceived to our hindsight and far ahead of its time. He pointed out an essential paradox of schizophrenia: that features of the illness lying closest to the core of the disease process (i.e., stable fundamental symptoms) are different from the features of illness that have been the focus of treatment (i.e., fluctuating accessory symptoms).

Clinical Symptoms

Bleuler's brilliant distinction and his emphasis on fundamental symptoms were downplayed for most of the twentieth century.

Accessory symptoms, such as hallucinations and delusions, became the elephant in the middle of the room. They were considered so dramatic that all other features of schizophrenia seemed small and faint in comparison. As a result, these psychotic symptoms became the basis for making a diagnosis. They still are—although with revisions to the diagnostic criteria, it is at least possible to meet a diagnosis of schizophrenia without hallucinations or delusions, as long as certain other symptoms are present (American Psychiatric Association, 1987). Other types of symptoms are also prominently found in schizophrenia, and over the last two decades, a broader view of the symptoms of schizophrenia has emerged. Instead of being listed separately like a shopping list, symptoms are typically grouped together in clusters. There are a variety of statistical procedures (such as factor analyses and principal components analyses) that help us to decide which symptoms group together naturally. Based on these types of analyses, it is now common to divide schizophrenia symptoms into three groups: positive psychotic, negative, and disorganized.

Positive Psychotic Symptoms

The most common positive psychotic symptoms are hallucinations and delusions. They are considered *positive* in the sense that they were not present to begin with, but emerged with the illness onset. As short hand, we will refer to positive psychotic symptoms simply as psychotic symptoms. Hallucinations in schizophrenia are typically auditory (i.e., hearing voices when there is no identifiable source). A patient with auditory hallucinations will hear voices that have a distinct auditory quality, and the experience is much like hearing actual voices. This experience is distinct from one's own thoughts. It is also different from trying to imagine a particular voice, such as the voice of a close friend. These auditory "images" do not have a true auditory quality. Perhaps closer to hallucinations is the sensation people sometimes have when they are startled by hearing "voices" when falling asleep or waking up. These are not really hallucinations either (patients experience hallucinations in a clear state of consciousness), but they are auditory experiences that may approximate the quality of the hallucination. Below are several first-person accounts of auditory hallucinations:

> I hear voices of abusively cruel people talking to me constantly, even when no one is present, and often such talk is a running commentary on every one of my daily activities. (Wagner, 1996, p. 400)

> I began to have hallucinations. At first, I thought they were spirits; I thought I heard angels and later, demons. Upon their arrival I felt no surprise; it seemed natural to me. I was not shocked, but was in awe. What sounded like baby angels was soothing; they sounded sweet and loving. They comforted me. But the demons were chilling, and I was terrified. (Murphy, 1997, p. 542)

> The voices are like people having a conversation inside my head of which I am not a part. They can be like scratching, whispers, or real loud, like shouting. They clutter my mind and I cannot think straight until I am unable to do anything. Sometimes they tell me to hurt others or myself. . . . When I first heard the voices, I would drink until I passed out. When I woke up with a vicious hangover, the voices would be there like thunder, and I would start drinking again. (Hummingbird, 1999, pp. 863–864)

Although auditory hallucinations are the most common, patients sometimes experience visual, tactile, olfactory (smell), or even gustatory (taste) hallucinations. By definition, all hallucinations (regardless of the type) occur in the absence of sensory stimulation. Seeing faces in clouds, or bodies in shadows, may be distressing, but they are illusions, not hallucinations. Seeing a face or person in detail against a plain wall is a visual hallucination.

Delusions are strange beliefs that are maintained despite evidence to the contrary. We can relate to some delusions, especially if they are within the realm of possibility (that is, nonbizarre). It is not uncommon for people to wonder if strangers are looking at them, or if someone has bad intentions toward them. Based on the available information, people will then decide whether to accept or reject the belief. The essence of a delusion is that nothing on earth can possibly convince delusional patients to change their belief; conviction is maintained, even in the face of contradictory evidence. Delusions may be based on possible situations, such as the idea that someone means them harm. Frequently, the delusions are bizarre, meaning that they are highly implausible or physically impossible. For example, one schizophrenic patient describes the following response to delusional thoughts:

> I came to believe that a local pharmacist was tormenting me by inserting his thoughts into my head, stealing mine, and inducing me to buy things I had no use for. The only way I could escape the influence of his deadly radiation was to walk a circuit a mile in diameter around his drugstore, and then I felt terrified and in terrible danger. (Wagner, 1996, p. 400)

When delusions are present, they are held with full conviction. Sometimes, however, delusions linger in a watered-down version when someone recovers from the illness. The following passage shows how the author gains insight into her delusion at the time she is writing about it, but is still unable to banish her delusional thoughts entirely:

> Although I had been raised Unitarian, without most of the usual Jewish or Christian beliefs, I became excessively preoccupied with religion. I began to misinterpret the everyday world, finding enormous and supernatural significance in apparent trifles. I knew I was evil, Satan's spawn, and to this day am not sure that I was not in fact responsible for JFK's assassination as well as other international catastrophes. (Wagner, 1996, p. 400)

Negative Symptoms

In the 1980s, the focus broadened to include symptoms other than the well-known psychotic symptoms. As opposed to psychotic symptoms that appear with the onset of illness, *negative* symptoms reflect the disappearance of certain abilities, emotions, and drives that are typically present. They reflect the absence of normal processes.

Negative symptoms include the absence of normal emotional expression in faces and gestures, reduction in normal thoughts and speech, and reduction in desire for social and familial connections. Negative symptoms have always been part of schizophrenia, but they are now much better appreciated. In the past, these symptoms may have been noticed but attributed to factors other than the illness.

Consider a frequently encountered situation. A set of parents have a son in his early twenties who previously had psychotic symptoms that are now well under control. His hallucinations are gone, and he no longer experiences delusional thinking. Despite these improvements, he spends his days sitting in front of the TV. The son seems unwilling to go back to school or look for a job, and, to make matters worse, he shows no interest in helping with basic household cleaning and chores. The parents, who were very understanding and supportive when he was hearing voices, become impatient and angry at their apparently lazy son. Why? Because they previously attributed the psychotic symptoms to the illness, but they now attribute the lack of motivation to sheer laziness. In fact, both of these are symptoms of schizophrenia. Not only are negative symptoms sometimes viewed as personality flaws instead of symptoms, they can also sound like depression, as seen in the statement below:

> I've also had many negative symptoms that make it extremely hard to motivate myself or perform any task or job. It has been hard to become interested in anything. Quite often, it has been very difficult to determine whether I am depressed or apathetic, a negative symptom. Whether labeled as negative symptoms or as depression, this lack of

interest and motivation has been a major problem for me. (Murphy, 1997, p. 542).

This patient's inability to enjoy and take interest in things is both a negative symptom of schizophrenia and a common feature of depression. It is difficult for a diagnostician to tease apart negative from depressive symptoms, and, as the author clearly notes, these features of schizophrenia are frustrating, regardless of what you call them.

Disorganized Symptoms

Disorganized speech (also called "formal thought disorder," or "conceptual disorganization") was once lumped together with psychotic symptoms. Statistical procedures have shown, however, that symptoms of disorganization usually "hang together" and form their own separate cluster. The symptoms include the loosening of associations (something Bleuler considered so important), in which patients have trouble forming coherent sentences because their thoughts skip from one idea to another. They might find themselves on an entirely different topic than the one they started, or taking a circuitous route to get there. For example, the following transcript (Marengo, Harrow, Lannin-Kettering, & Wilson, 1985) is an interpretation by a patient concerning the saying, "When the cat's away, the mice will play":

> If something has to do with freedom to do with something you want to do. When they're gone you can do whatever it is. Do you want it another way? When something is injured or you have been injured, then you aren't like you were catching mice. (p. 429)

Sometimes the statements of patients include words that are made-up or meaningful only to the individual. These idiosyncratic words are called neologisms. In response to the saying, "Don't swap horses in the middle of a stream," one patient said:

That's *wish-bell.* Double vision. It's like walking across a person's eye and reflecting personality. It works on you, like dying and going to the spiritual world, but landing in the *Vella* world. (Marengo et al., 1985, p. 423)

Like poetry from the beat generation, the statements of patients wander in a loosely connected way. It is sometimes tempting to look for meaning in the thin strands that hold the statements together. But patients do not intend this to be poetry. They are having difficulty grabbing on to a single topic. One patient describes his difficulty in organizing his thoughts:

My thoughts get all jumbled up. I start thinking or talking about something but I never get there. Instead, I wander off in the wrong direction and get caught up with all sorts of different things that may be connected with things I want to say but in a way I can't explain. People listening to me get more lost than I do. (McGhie & Chapman, 1961, p. 108)

Diagnosis

Schizophrenia is a disease without a diagnostic test. No existing blood test, urine test, or biopsy can make a definitive diagnosis of schizophrenia, and it is unlikely that any such test will be available in the near future. The neurocognitive tests and brain scans described in this book are not routinely given to patients and at this time are mainly used for research purposes; although abnormalities on such tests are associated with schizophrenia, they do not help one arrive at a diagnosis. Despite the dazzling advances in the biomedical sciences, the diagnosis for schizophrenia is made the old-fashioned way—in an office with a skilled clinician asking questions and scribbling down notes as the patient describes his or her experiences. Even diagnosis by interview is not straightforward because there is no one symptom that is specific to schizophrenia; nor is there any symptom that "rules out" schizophrenia. The diagnosis of schizophrenia rests on a constellation of features detailed in the 4th edition of the

---

Table 1.1 *Abbreviated Diagnostic Criteria for Schizophrenia*

A. Characteristic Symptoms: At least two or more for a significant portion of a 1-month period
    1) delusions
    2) hallucinations
    3) disorganized speech
    4) grossly disorganized or catatonic behavior
    5) negative symptoms

B. Social & Occupational Dysfunction: At least one of the following areas:
    1) work
    2) interpersonal relations
    3) self-care

C. Duration: 6 months continuously and at least one month of active symptoms (criteria A)

D. Schizoaffective and Mood Disorder exclusion

E. Substance/General Medical Condition exclusion

F. Pervasive Developmental Disorder exclusion

Diagnostic and Statistical Manual (*DSM-IV*) (American Psychiatric Association, 1994). Diagnostic criteria for schizophrenia are listed in abbreviated form in Table 1.1. We will cover some of the main categories necessary for a diagnosis of schizophrenia.

Characteristic Symptoms

During the active phase of illness, some of the three types of symptoms discussed above need to be present. They include psychotic symptoms (hallucinations and delusions), negative symptoms (social withdrawal, affective blunting), and disorganized symptoms (disorganized speech). In addition to these major types of symptoms, there is a category for behavioral abnormalities, including disorganized and catatonic behaviors. Grossly disorganized behavior can include silliness, extreme agitation, or self-neglect of food or hygiene. Catatonia refers to a decreased reactivity to the environment such as being unaware of one's surroundings or maintaining a fixed and rigid position.

For a diagnosis of schizophrenia, the patient needs to have active clinical symptoms from Section A for a significant portion of a 1-month period. It is technically possible for patients to meet criteria for the active phase without psychotic symptoms, but it is exceedingly rare. For the most part, the active part of the illness is defined by hallucinations and/or delusions, although they are frequently accompanied by negative and disorganized symptoms.

Functional Impairment

The threshold for a diagnosis of schizophrenia is set intentionally high, and it requires functional impairment. Schizophrenia is an unwelcome and burdensome diagnosis; consequently it should be given conservatively. A diagnosis of schizophrenia requires some dysfunction in interpersonal relations, work or education, or self-care. If a person functions as well as ever, without a deterioration in work, school, family, and peer relationships, then that person does not have schizophrenia, no matter how many times he or she hears voices.

> My relationships with others are, at best, very loose. I recently read in a brochure that people with schizophrenia have difficulty making and keeping friends, which has definitely been true in my case. I have given up on the idea of getting married and having children someday. Instead, I have decided to devote my life to writing. (Dykstra, 1997, p. 698)

Duration

Another way to set a high threshold is to require a certain duration of illness. For schizophrenia, the requirement is that the person be continuously ill for at least 6 months. That does not mean that he or she has fully active symptoms for the entire period. It is necessary to have at least 1 month of the active symptoms. The remainder of the period could involve milder versions of the symptoms called residual symptoms.

Differential Diagnosis

One of the hardest aspects of making a diagnosis of schizophrenia is making sure it's not something else. For example, schizophrenia can look like (1) mania in its active phase, (2) depression with psychotic features, (3) certain forms of drug abuse, (4) extreme obsessive compulsive disorder, and (5) posttraumatic stress disorder, just to name a few. There is also a separate disorder, Schizoaffective Disorder, that specifically has features of both schizophrenia and mood disorder. Historically, this disorder has swung back and forth, sometimes classified as a variant of mood disorder and sometimes as a variant of schizophrenia. It has aptly been called the Alsace Lorraine of psychiatry.

The *DSM* criteria are taken quite seriously, but they are intentionally left vague in some places. Terms such as "relatively brief duration" or "a significant portion of a 1-month period" are stated without clear definition. This ambiguity creates the need for judgment calls and esoteric discussions. Many people would be surprised to see a group of diagnosticians discussing interpretation of phrases from the *DSM* with a seriousness and passion that is comparable to a group of rabbis discussing interpretation of phrases from the Torah.

Consider the following examples from a psychiatric casebook (Spitzer, Gibbon, Skodol, Williams, & First, 1989). Some of the examples may seem like schizophrenia, but only one is. Identifying information in these case studies has been changed to maintain confidentiality.

Dear Doctor

Myrna Field, a 55-year-old woman, was a cashier in a hospital coffee shop three years ago when she suddenly developed the belief that a physician who dropped in regularly was intensely in love with her. She fell passionately in love with him, but said nothing and became increasingly distressed each time she saw him. Casual remarks that he made were interpreted as cues to his feelings, and she believed he gave her significant glances and made suggestive movements, though he never declared his feelings openly. She was sure this was because he was married.

After more than two years of this, she became so agitated that she had to give up her job; she remained at home, thinking about the physician incessantly. When she was interviewed, Myrna was very distressed, and talked under great pressure. Her intelligence was limited, and many of her ideas appeared simple; but the only clear abnormality was the unshakeable belief that her physician "lover" was passionately devoted to her. She could not be persuaded otherwise.

In the case of Myrna, her only psychotic symptom is a firm and disruptive delusion that a particular doctor was in love with her. The lone symptom does not meet criteria for schizophrenia, because at least two symptoms are required from the "A" category. Interestingly, she has functional impairment as a result of her single symptom. A single nonbizarre delusion like this is consistent with a diagnosis of Delusional Disorder. She responded to antipsychotic medication.

Radar Messages

Alice Davis, a 24-year-old copy editor, comes to a psychiatrist for help in continuing her treatment with a mood stabilizer, lithium. She describes how, three years previously, she was a successful college student in her senior year, doing well academically and enjoying a large circle of friends of both sexes. In the midst of an uneventful period in the first semester, she began to feel depressed; experienced loss of appetite, with a weight loss of about ten pounds; and had both trouble falling asleep and waking up too early.

After about two months of these problems, they seemed to go away; but she then began to feel increasingly energetic, requiring only two to five hours' sleep at night, and to experience her thoughts as "racing." She started to see symbolic meanings in things, especially sexual meanings, and began to suspect that innocent comments on television shows were referring to her. Over the next month, she became increasingly euphoric, irritable, and over talkative. She started to believe that there was a hole in her head through which radar messages were being sent to her. These messages could control her thoughts or produce emotions of anger, sadness, or the like, that were beyond her control. She also believed that her thoughts could be read by people around her and that alien thoughts from other people were intruding themselves via the radar into her own head. She described hearing voices, which some· times spoke about her in the third person and at other times ordered her to perform various acts, particularly sexual ones.

Her friends, concerned about Alice's unusual behavior, took her to an emergency room, where she was evaluated and admitted to a psychiatric unit. After a day of observation, Alice was started on an antipsychotic, chlorpromazine, and lithium carbonate. Over the course of about three weeks, she experienced a fairly rapid reduction in all of the symptoms that had brought her to the hospital.

Approximately eight months after her discharge, Alice was taken off lithium carbonate by the psychiatrist in the college mental health clinic. She continued to do fairly well for the next few months, but then began to experience a gradual reappearance of symptoms similar to those that had necessitated her hospitalization. The symptoms worsened, and after two weeks she was readmitted to the hospital with almost the identical symptoms that she had had when first admitted.

Alice responded in days to chlorpromazine and lithium; and, once again, the chlorpromazine was gradually discontinued, leaving her on lithium alone. . . . For the past year, while continuing to take lithium, she has been symptom free and functioning fairly well, getting a job in publishing and recently moving to New York to advance her career.

Alice clearly has psychotic symptoms (believing that radar messages were sent through a hole in her head and hearing voices), and the clinician needs to decide which psychotic disorder to diagnose. Because her psychotic symptoms are limited to the period of time that she was experiencing mania, a diagnosis of schizophrenia is ruled out (criteria in Section D are not met). Instead she is diagnosed with a mood disorder (Bipolar Disorder because it includes periods of both depression and mania) with psychotic features.

Sam Schaefer

A psychiatrist was asked by the court to evaluate a 21-year-old man arrested in a robbery since his lawyer raised the issue of his competence to stand trial. During the course of a two-and-a-half-hour evaluation, the patient acknowledged frequent run-ins with the law since about the age of 11 and incarceration in various institutions for criminal offenses, but was reluctant to provide details about them.

During the interview he appeared calm and in control, sat slouched in the chair, and had good eye contact. His affect showed a good range. His thought processes were logical, sequential, and spontaneous even when he was describing many difficulties with his thinking. He seemed guarded in his answers, particularly to questions about his psychological symptoms.

He claims to have precognition on occasion, knowing, for instance, what is going to be served for lunch in the jail;

that people hear his thoughts, as if broadcast on the radio; and that he does not like narcotics because Jeane Dixon doesn't like narcotics either, and she is in control of his thoughts. He states that he has seen a vision of General Lee in his cell, and that his current incarceration is a mission in which he is attempting to be an undercover agent for the police, although none of the local police realize this. He says that "Sam Schaefer" is his "case name."

When asked the date, he said that it was June 28, either 1970 or 1985. He then saw the inconsistency in the dates he gave for the year and said that this therefore must be 1978, since he was 20 and was born in 1958. . . . Asked to do additions, he responded: $4 + 6 = 10$, $4 + 3 = 7$, $4 + 8 = 14$.

When asked the color of the red rug in the room, he said it was orange; his blue and white striped shirt he said was white on white. When presented with some questions from an aphasia screening test, he copied a square faithfully except for rounding the corners; a cross was copied as a capital "I." When shown a picture of a clock, he said he did not know what it was, but it looked familiar. A dinner fork was identified as a "pitchfork."

When asked whether he thought he was competent to stand trial, he replied, "yes," and said he did not think that there was anything wrong with him mentally. When told that the examiner agreed with his assessment, he thought for several seconds and then, somewhat angered, protested that he probably couldn't cooperate with his attorney because he couldn't remember things very well, and therefore was incompetent to stand trial.

Superficially, this person meets the "A" criteria of schizophrenia, but the description of the symptoms raises doubts in the interviewer's mind. The "psychotic" symptoms appear to be under voluntary control. The person reports a large number of unrelated delusions, but does so in an unusually coherent manner. Cognitive deficits are common in schizophrenia, but they appear highly exaggerated in this man (e.g., not knowing the color of the rug), especially considering that his speech is clear and organized. The avoidance of prosecution is a strong motivation for him to appear insane. His diagnosis is Malingering.

Under Surveillance

Mr. Simpson is a 44-year-old, single, unemployed, white man brought into the emergency room by the police for striking an elderly woman in his apartment building. His chief complaint is, "That damn bitch. She and the rest of them deserved more than that for what they put me through."

Mr. Simpson had been continually ill since the age of 22. During his first year of law school, he gradually became more and more convinced that his classmates were making fun of him. He noticed that they would snort and sneeze whenever he entered the classroom. When a girl he was dating broke off the relationships with him, he believed that she had been "replaced" by a look-alike. He called the police and asked for their help to solve the "kidnapping." His academic performance in school declined dramatically, and he was asked to leave and seek psychiatric care.

Mr. Simpson got a job as an investment counselor at a bank, which he held for seven months. However, he was getting an increasing number of distracting "signals" from co-workers, and he became more and more suspicious and withdrawn. It was at this time that he first reported hearing voices. He was eventually fired, and soon thereafter was hospitalized for the first time, at age 24. He has not worked since.

Mr. Simpson has been hospitalized 12 times, the longest stay being eight months. However, in the last five years he has been hospitalized only once, for three weeks. During the hospitalizations he has received various antipsychotic drugs. Although outpatient medication has been prescribed, he usually stops taking it shortly after leaving the hospital. Aside from twice-yearly lunch meetings with his uncle and his contacts with mental health workers, he is totally isolated socially. He lives on his own and manages his own financial affairs, including a modest inheritance. He reads the *Wall Street Journal* daily. He cooks and cleans for himself.

Mr. Simpson maintains that his apartment is the center of a large communication system that involves all three major television networks, his neighbors, and apparently hundreds of "actors" in his neighborhood. There are secret cameras in his apartment that carefully monitor all his activities. When he is watching TV, many of his minor actions (e.g., getting up to go to the bathroom) are soon directly commented on by the announcer. Whenever he goes outside, the "actors" have all been warned to keep him under surveillance. Everyone on the street watches him. His neighbors operate two different "machines"; one is responsible for all of his voices, except the "joker." He is not certain who controls this voice, which "visits" him only occasionally, and is very funny.

Mr. Simpson describes other unusual experiences. For example, he recently went to a shoe store 30 miles from his house in the hope of getting some shoes that wouldn't be "altered." However, he soon found out that, like the rest of the shoes he buys, special nails had been put into the bottom of the shoes to annoy him. He was amazed that his decision concerning which shoe store to go to must have been known to his "harassers" before he himself knew it, so that they had time to get the altered shoes made up especially for him. He realizes that great effort and "millions of dollars" are involved in keeping him under surveillance. He sometimes thinks this is all part of a large experiment to discover the secret of his "superior intelligence."

Mr. Simpson has characteristic symptoms of schizophrenia. He has delusions of reference (that classmates are making fun of him), paranoid delusions (that his neighbors are actually actors and his thoughts are monitored), grandiose delusions (he is under surveillance due to his superior intelligence), and auditory hallucinations. His delusions are fairly well organized, and he appears to be able to present them in a clear manner. He unambiguously meets the "A" criteria. He also has functional impairment (Section B). He is unable to work and is socially isolated, though he is able to live independently and maintain activities of daily living. Because the illness is of long duration (Section C) and not related to mood disorder, substance abuse, or other disorders (Sections D, E, and F), his diagnosis is schizophrenia.

How can we start to understand the experience of Mr. Simpson? To make sense of this illness, we need to grasp what goes wrong in the brain and what goes wrong in the community. This book will revolve around three key aspects of schizophrenia: neural connections, neurocognitive deficits, and functional impairment. Our understanding of each of these aspects has grown considerably in the last decade. Schizophrenia is essentially a disorder of neural connections, and these neural problems lead to neurocognitive deficits. The neurocognitive deficits lead, in turn, to misinterpretations and confusion, and eventually to functional impairment. In the next chapter, we will look at the problem in terms of the development of the nervous system. As we will see, neurons in schizophrenia are not great communicators.

Chapter Two

Development of Schizophrenia

When Does It Start?

One of the most perplexing aspects of schizophrenia is how it develops. For some individuals, the onset of the illness seems to occur suddenly in early adulthood. For others, the onset follows a long period of subtle behavioral problems (called the prodrome). Differences in the way schizophrenia emerges are strikingly variable. In an effort to understand this variability, scientists have tried to understand the processes that kick off the first episode. The focus has been on the onset—the crucial moment when a person crosses the threshold from normality to psychosis. Unappreciated until recently was that the onset of illness is not really the beginning of the illness at all; it is the final step on a very long path. For schizophrenia, it is necessary to think in terms of *risk* or *predisposition* as opposed to onset. Once we start looking for risk factors, we find that they can start very early in life.

People are born with a certain genetic predisposition for schizophrenia. Some have more of a predisposition than others, and there are no guarantees as to who will develop the disease. Whether or not schizophrenia develops depends not only on the person's genetic predisposition but also on risk factors that increase the chance of developing schizophrenia and on protective factors that decrease the chance. Risk factors for schizophrenia are akin to striking out in baseball: One needs to accumulate a certain number of strikes, and the exact number depends on the amount of one's predisposition. People who have experienced some risk factors for schizophrenia will not develop the illness if they can avoid accumulating the requisite number of "strikes" for their level of predisposition.

In this chapter, we will start to review how problems at the neuron level translate into features of schizophrenia seen in the adult patient. Some of the steps (depicted in figure 2.1), including problems in neurodevelopment and problems in connections among neurons, will be discussed in this chapter. Later chapters will explore other steps shown in the figure, including vulnerability to schizophrenia, neurocognitive deficits, and functional impairment.

Studying early risk factors in schizophrenia is difficult because research usually begins when a person already has schizophrenia and is typically in his or her thirties or forties. Yet the risk factors have occurred decades earlier. To explore such factors scientifically, we need some objective way to look back in time. Several creative approaches that have been used to explore early risk factors are discussed below.

Approaches for Exploring Neurodevelopment in Schizophrenia

Population Studies

Clues about origins of schizophrenia have come from rather unlikely sources. Consider what we learned about the illness from historical events around World War II. On the last day of November 1939, the Soviet Union invaded Finland and started what has become known as the Winter War of 1939. The invasion force, estimated at over 1 million men, greatly outnumbered the Finnish defenders, and the Soviets expected a swift and crushing victory. The Soviet forces encountered remarkably stiff resistance from the Finns, however, and the invasion stalled. Unusually bitter winter conditions worked to the benefit of the Finnish troops—who moved easily on skis and were well suited for winter

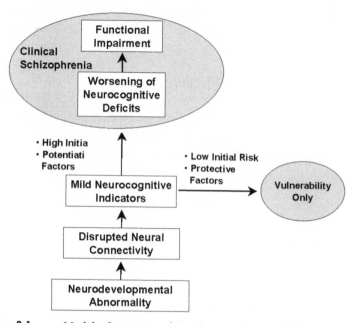

Figure 2.1 ■ *Model of steps to schizophrenia. This model shows the hypothesized steps from neurodevelopmental abnormality to clinical schizophrenia. Note that not all of the individuals with vulnerability develop clinical schizophrenia; it depends on protective and potentiating factors.*

battle conditions—but not to the benefit of the lumbering Soviet tank columns. In a lasting reminder of the conflict, the name of the Soviet foreign minister was indelibly attached to a Finnish battle tactic: Finnish troops learned to stop advancing Soviet tanks by throwing lighted bottles of fuel (Molotov cocktails) into the turrets. Despite the heroic stand of the Finns, the Soviets reinforced, reorganized, and eventually accomplished their territorial goals. After 3½ months, the Winter War of 1939 ended with high casualties on both sides.

Now for the connection to schizophrenia: Roughly 25,000 Finnish soldiers lost their lives in the conflict with the Soviets. Some of these soldiers left behind wives who were pregnant, and some left behind wives with children under the age of 1 year. The two groups of offspring differed in their risk for schizophrenia. The group that was in utero when their mothers learned that their fathers were killed had a higher rate of schizophrenia as adults (Huttunen & Niskanen, 1978). The family trauma was extreme for both types of offspring, but the implications for development are quite different. For the offspring in utero, their nervous system was still in a critical phase of development. In contrast, the offspring who were young children had a more complete nervous system that was much less susceptible to disruption. This naturalistic study has two implications: first, that early development of the nervous system (i.e., neurodevelopment) is critically linked to schizophrenia. Second, factors that disrupt early neurodevelopment may increase the risk for developing schizophrenia.

Neurodevelopment is organized into several phases, some of which may be especially critical to the development of schizophrenia. Another study from Finland identified a particularly important stage of neurodevelopment. In the fall of 1957, Helsinki experienced an A2 influenza epidemic. Influenza is not uncommon in Helsinki, but the epidemic of 1957 was unusual in two respects. First, it was relatively brief, with clear start and end dates. The flu started on October 8th and ended five weeks later, on November 14th. Second, it was fairly widespread. As much as two thirds of the city's population may have experienced some signs of infection.

A study tested the possibility that exposure to the influenza virus during pregnancy could increase the risk for schizophrenia in the offspring (Mednick, Machon, Huttunen, & Bonett, 1988). Researchers determined the adult rates of schizophrenia in offspring who were in utero during the influenza epidemic of 1957 and compared these rates to those of control individuals. Each trimester of pregnancy was looked at separately. Offspring who were born during the 3 months after the epidemic were in their third trimester at the time of the epidemic. Those born 4 to 6 months after the epidemic were in their second trimester at the time of the epidemic, and those born 7 to 9 months afterwards were in their first trimester. As a control, the researchers looked at rates of schizophrenia in individuals born in the same hospitals during the same months of previous years.

The rates of schizophrenia differed according to when the offspring were exposed to the virus. For offspring who were exposed during the first and third trimesters, the rates of schizophrenia were nearly the same as those of the control subjects. But for those exposed during the second trimester of pregnancy, the rates of schizophrenia were much greater.

Numerous studies have examined influenza epidemics from other geographic regions. Most, but not all, of these studies have shown increased risk of schizophrenia with exposure to influenza during the second trimester (Barr, Mednick, & Munck-Jorgenson, 1990; O'Callaghan, Sham, Takei, Glover, & Murray, 1991). Based on these studies, researchers have concluded that a virus such as influenza can disrupt neurodevelopment in the second trimester, and that this disruption is linked to the eventual development of schizophrenia (Murray, Jones, O'Callaghan, Takei, & Sham, 1992; Weinberger, 1995).

How could a virus in the mother increase risk in the fetus? One possibility is that the mother may produce antibodies in response to a virus, and these antibodies might affect the fetus. A more direct way to examine the role of maternal antibodies is to consider the effects of Rhesus (Rh) incompatibility. During the second trimester, a transfer of maternal antibodies from mother to fetus occurs. Incompatibility of the RhD antigen (RhD-negative mother/RhD-positive infant) can cause hemolytic disease and brain damage in the fetus. A RhD-negative mother generally develops RhD antibodies following her first pregnancy with a RhD-positive infant, so that incompatibility is not usually a problem for the firstborn Rh-positive infant. In a study of individuals born in Denmark between 1959 and 1961, the rates of schizophrenia were compared for Rh compatible and incompatible groups (Hollister, Laing, & Mednick, 1996). The rates of schizophrenia were nearly three times greater when RhD-negative mothers gave birth to RhD-positive offspring, compared with those who were RhD compatible. Not only does this study suggest a specific mechanism of increased risk for schizophrenia, it also indicates that some risk factors are preventable because the effects of Rh incompatibility can be effectively treated (Wyatt, 1996).

Starvation is also a risk factor for schizophrenia. Another population study from World War II illustrates the impact of starvation during the first trimester. By September of 1944, the Allies had invaded France and crossed two branches of the Rhine River, but they were unable to capture key bridges that connected the Netherlands to Germany. (This unsuccessful effort was described in Cornelius Ryan's book, *A Bridge Too Far*, later made into a movie.) Dutch railroad workers went on strike to support the Allies, and the Germans retaliated by imposing a blockade of western Holland. The result was severe famine for this region from October 1944 until the end of the war in May 1945. The famine, which became known as the Dutch Hunger Winter, reached its peak from February to April 1945, during which time bread and potatoes formed nearly the entire ration. Researchers followed the offspring of women who were pregnant during the Hunger Winter to examine whether starvation increased the development of subsequent psychiatric disorders (Susser et al., 1996; Susser & Lin, 1992). The offspring of women exposed to severe famine during their first trimester of pregnancy had about a two-fold increase in rates of hospitalization for schizophrenia. It appears that some risk factors such as influenza and Rh compatibility exert their effects mainly during the second trimester, but for unknown reasons, starvation has its effects slightly earlier in development.

During the past decade, one of the major discoveries about schizophrenia is that prenatal factors can influence risk for the illness. However, it would be wrong to conclude from these studies that influenza, starvation, or similar factors *cause* schizophrenia in the offspring. Instead, they are factors that increase one's risk—they do not predetermine the illness. Prenatal factors interact with genetic predisposition and other risk and protective factors in such a way that it is impossible to predict whether any one person will eventually develop schizophrenia.

These types of risk factors probably account for a small minority of patients with schizophrenia. Recall that schizophrenia affects about 1 percent of the population. Even if we assume that influenza exposure in the second trimester doubles the risk for schizophrenia, it still means that only a small percentage of these mothers (about 2 percent) might give birth to a child who later develops the illness. Also, how can we explain the vast majority of schizophrenic patients who were not exposed to an obvious risk factor during the second trimester? Genetic factors must also be key for development of schizophrenia. In the population studies just discussed, we are probably seeing an interaction between a genetic predisposition and nongenetic risk factors. An individual might be predisposed to schizophrenia, but in the absence of any risk factor, schizophrenia will not develop. For other predisposed individuals, influenza during the second trimester, or starvation during the first, might make the difference between having schizophrenia and only being predisposed to it. The importance of finding such risk factors is not that they explain most cases of schizophrenia but that they identify a specific time in development and specific factors that may increase risk for schizophrenia.

Identification of risk factors can eventually lead to prevention strategies. Knowing key risk factors helps to identify individuals who are at heightened risk for the illness and who may benefit from psychosocial support to reduce the impact of subsequent risk factors. Also, some of the risk factors mentioned, including Rh compatibility and starvation, are targets of public health programs that could reduce rates of severe mental illness in offspring. Schizophrenia is not the only psychiatric disorder linked to early prenatal factors. Studies have found that affective disorders (such as depression and mania) are also linked to starvation and influenza during the prenatal period (Brown, van Os, Driessens, Hoek, & Susser, 2000; Machon, Mednick, & Huttunen, 1997). Because these risk factors are not limited to schizophrenia, their control and prevention may have broader public health significance.

The idea of prenatal risk factors influencing mental health is not new. Consider the following statement, written roughly 2,000 years ago in a Chinese medical text called the *Yellow Emperor's Classic of Internal Medicine*:

People are born to have the illness of craziness, how does it come about? . . . it is an illness started in the womb, resulting from a bad scare of the mother when she was pregnant. (translated in Lam & Berrios, 1992)

Ideas that have been circulating in the form of folk wisdom for millennia are receiving experimental support for the first time.

Archival Approach: Home Movies

Imagine that you have a son, daughter, brother, or sister with schizophrenia. If you could go back in time and see your child or sibling again, before they were ill, would you notice any signs that would point to future mental illness? What would you notice? In the following passage, a photo serves as a correction on the memories of a sibling whose brother developed schizophrenia.

Despite the differences in the way we perceived and coped with the world, Andy and I were unusually close as children. His presence in my life and mine in his was more constant than that of either of our parents. I adored and emulated my older brother, tagged after him, and vied for his attention; he was my daily companion, my playmate, and so I believed, my protector.

However, a recent look at old family photos has given my memories a jolt, and made me question who was really protecting whom. Paradoxically, these snapshots belie my memories of Andy as my caretaker. In each and every one, I stand in the foreground with Andy several paces behind me, even though he is older by a year-and-a-half and there are only two of us in the picture. I am sturdy and smiling; Andy is frail, his handsome features scrunched up into a scowl. He holds his body in an odd, concave position, sucking in the center of his body, with his head pitched awkwardly forward. Thin arms, bent at the elbows, hang lank behind his torso as if he holds onto a set of invisible supporting bars. Occasionally, he smiles, but these pictures are the most disturbing of all: My brother's taut, clenched smile, baring most of his upper and lower front teeth, conveys only great tension and pain: it is a frozen, sound-less scream. (Brodoff, 1998, pp. 114–115)

Similarly, home movies can serve as a unique type of database. Frequently, families with a schizophrenic son or daughter also have a child who does not develop the illness. Studies conducted by Elaine Walker and colleagues have used home movies to study childhood precursors of schizophrenia (Walker, Grimes, Davis, & Smith, 1993; Walker, Savoie, & Davis, 1994). In these studies, researchers obtained home movies from families who had a child with schizophrenia and at least one child who did not develop the illness. Since parents often take movies of their children during certain events (e.g., the first birthday, the first steps), the siblings can be compared in roughly similar situations. When raters were asked to identify the pre-schizophrenic child in these home movies, they were generally accurate. The pre-schizophrenic child usually differed from the control sibling in a couple of ways. First, the pre-schizophrenic child often showed more negative emotions compared with the control sibling (for example, crying when coming in contact with adults). Second, the child frequently had unusual motoric features such as awkward movements. Figure 2.2 is a frame from a home movie in which a pre-schizo-phrenic child displays atypical hand posture.

Home movies provide convincing evidence that abnormali-ties in development are revealed early in life, though not as clinical symptoms or any of the more typical features of schiz-ophrenia. Rather, early problems are reflected as behavioral abnormalities in motor and emotional development. Interestingly, motor abnormalities are most noticeable in the first couple of years and then become less prominent as the child develops; these early warning signs seem to emerge and then submerge, but not entirely. For example, carefully collected records from draft boards indicate that problems are detectable in male pre-schizophrenic adolescents. Studies of army conscripts in Sweden and Israel reveal reduced cognitive

Figure 2.2 ■ *Picture of a pre-schizophrenic boy. This photo shows an unusual arm and hand posture in an individual who will later develop schizophrenia. Such motoric abnormalities are more common in pre-schizophrenic children than in their siblings. From Walker, 1994. Courtesy of Elaine Walker.*

and intellectual abilities, as well as reduced social functioning, years before onset of the illness (David, Malmberg, Brandt, Allebeck, & Lewis, 1997; Davidson et al., 1999). Next, we will consider whether signs of abnormal development are also observable in adult patients.

Examining Markers of Abnormal Development

Yogi Berra once said that you can see a lot just by observing. We all carry subtle "recordings" of our neurodevelopment—we just need to know where to look. If we observe closely in schizophrenia, we can find markers of abnormal neurodevelopment, including minor physical anomalies, unusual fingerprints (dermatoglyphics), neurological soft signs, and atypical handedness.

Minor physical anomalies. Over 100 years ago, Thomas Clouston, a professor from the University of Edinburgh in

Scotland, identified a subgroup of psychotic patients who were characterized by a deformed palate and other signs of abnormal development (cited in Murray & Jones, 1995). He astutely concluded that the deformed palate was a permanent marker linked to abnormal development of the nervous system. Indeed, modern studies have shown that subtle physical abnormalities, called minor physical anomalies, or MPAs, can be observed in a subgroup of patients.

MPAs are minor abnormalities of the head, feet, hands, and face (e.g., high-steepled palate, large or small distance between tear ducts, malformed ears, or webbing between the toes). Examples of two MPAs (eye fold and large distance between the eyes) are shown in figure 2.3. Don't worry if you have some of these—normal people often have MPAs, though usually not more than a couple. MPAs are thought to reflect indirectly the development of the central nervous system. First, MPAs and the nervous system both derive from the same embryonic layer. Second, high rates of MPAs are associated with disorders that have clear prenatal neural involvement (e.g., Down's Syndrome). MPAs likely reflect processes in the second trimester of neurodevelopment (Green, Bracha, Satz, & Christenson, 1994), a time frame that fits well with the population studies discussed earlier.

If schizophrenia involves abnormal development of the nervous system, then individuals with schizophrenia should have an excess of MPAs; and indeed, they do (Green, Satz, & Christenson, 1994; Green, Satz, Gaier, Ganzell, & Kharabi, 1989; Guy, Majorski, Wallace, & Guy, 1983; O'Callaghan, Larkin, Kinsella, & Waddington, 1991). MPAs in schizophrenia occur in many different body regions and include subtle abnormalities of the ears, eyes, mouth, as well as both large and small head circumferences.

Fingerprints (dermatoglyphics). Dermatoglyphics (literally, skin carvings) are finger-, hand-, and footprints. People are well aware that everyone has unique fingerprints and this uniqueness makes them valuable for identification. But, dermatoglyphics can also be used as a subtle record of neurodevelopment. Ridges on the fingers are set down between weeks 14 and 22 of gestation,

Figure 2.3 ▪ *MPAs. This photo shows minor eye abnormalities (eye fold and wide-set eyes) in a Caucasian girl. From Waldrop & Halverson, 1971.*

so any events that occur during this time are likely to be reflected in a subtle disruption of the print pattern. Like fossils of neurodevelopment, dermatoglyphics provide records of developmental events, but few details.

A key measure from dermatoglyphics is the total number of ridges on each finger (see figure 2.4). Schizophrenic patients show two types of abnormalities. One subgroup of patients has fewer ridges, perhaps because they had a reduced blood supply during development. A second subgroup showed more ridges, perhaps due to swelling (edema) during the second trimester (Bracha, Torrey, Bigelow, Lohr, & Linington, 1991; Bracha, Torrey, Gottesman, Bigelow, & Cunniff, 1992; Davis & Bracha, 1996). Individuals with schizophrenia also show higher variability in ridge counts between the left and right hands, called fluctuating asymmetry, which indicates a disturbance in fetal neurodevelopment (Markow & Gottesman, 1989; Mellor, 1992).

The dermatoglyphic abnormalities are most clear in studies of identical twins who are discordant for schizophrenia (one twin has schizophrenia and the other does not). Usually, identical twins are highly similar in their number of ridges. However, figure 2.4 demonstrates that this is not the case when one twin has schizophrenia. To count ridges, a line is first drawn between two landmarks on the print (the lines start in the lower left corner of each print). The number of ridges that cross the line is the ridge count. In figure 2.4, the healthy twin has almost twice the ridge count of the affected twin (20 vs. 11). This difference indicates that their lives in the womb were far from identical, even though they are genetically identical. The lower ridge count suggests that the affected twin may have experienced some reduction in blood and nutrient supply.

Healthy Twin   Schizophrenic Twin

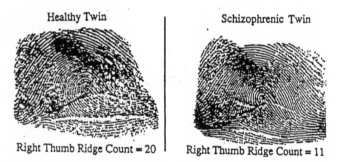

Right Thumb Ridge Count = 20   Right Thumb Ridge Count = 11

Figure 2.4 ■ *Dermatoglyphics. These fingerprints are from a pair of monozygotic (identical) twins who are discordant for schizophrenia. The healthy twin, on the left, has a much larger ridge count than the affected twin. To determine ridge counts, a line is drawn according to landmarks (starting in the lower left corner of each print), and the number of ridges that cross the line are counted. From Bracha et al., 1992.*

Atypical handedness and neurological soft signs. Problems in neurodevelopment during the prenatal period may well be reflected in delays or abnormalities in development during early childhood. Just as home movies sometimes indicate a lag in motor development in pre-schizophrenic children, simple neurological examinations administered to adult schizophrenic patients can reveal problems in the development of the nervous system. Many of these neurological abnormalities are not as pronounced as those associated with severe neurological conditions (e.g., abnormal reflexes and loss of sensation). Instead, they are minor indicators called "soft" neurological signs (Flashman, Flaum, Gupta, & Andreasen, 1996; Ismail, Cantor-Graae, & McNeil, 1998). For example, when a child performs a task with one hand, he or she sometimes makes similar unintended movements in the other hand (a mirror movement). Such a movement is normal for a child, but in an adult it is considered to be a soft neurological sign. Related to these soft signs are problems in establishing handedness.

Hand preference is a very simple behavioral index, but it can be informative. Atypical handedness distributions (usually caused by increased rates of left-handedness) are seen in a variety of disorders such as autism, mental retardation, epilepsy, and stroke. As a group, schizophrenic patients show less right-handedness than the general population. Initially, this finding was interpreted to mean that schizophrenia, like other developmental disorders, had a high rate of left-handedness. However, the shift in hand preference is an unusual one—it is a shift away from right-handedness, but not an increase in left-handedness. Instead, the shift is largely due to an increase in atypical, or "ambiguous," handedness, in which hand preference is not as firm as it should be. Rates of atypical handedness, which are only about 2 percent in a normal sample, can be around 20 percent in a group of schizophrenic individuals. A relatively high percentage of patients switch hands, not only when performing different tasks (e.g., writing with their right hand and throwing with their left) but also by using different hands when asked to repeat the same activity (Green, Satz, Smith, & Nelson, 1989; Satz & Green, 1999). The atypical handedness, like MPAs and unusual dermatoglyphics, is another indication of neurodevelopment gone slightly awry. In the next section, we discuss what aberrant neurodevelopment means from the neuron's point of view.

Examining the Development of Neural Connections

The prenatal period, in particular the second trimester, appears to be a critical time of risk for schizophrenia. The second trimester is also the time when neurons travel to their destinations in order to set up connections with other neurons. This process is called *cell migration.*

To grasp the importance of disruption in cell migration, imagine a mythical city of brightly colored houses. The city's furniture factory creates brightly colored items to match the brightly colored houses. The factory receives orders from houses, makes the furniture, packs it in boxes, and then transports it to the correct address. When all is going well, green furniture arrives at a green house, blue furniture arrives at a blue house, and everything is in place. Now imagine a relatively minor problem—the driver of the truck carrying the furniture has a poor sense of distance and direction. As a result, boxes of furniture are delivered to a neighboring house instead of to the one that ordered it. Green furniture ends up at the red house, blue furniture in a yellow house, and so on. To make matters worse, the minor transportation problem generates confusion among the locals. The households are not sure about their identity (do we belong to a green or blue family?), they are not sure what to order next (what colors should the drapes be?), and they are not sure what to make of their neighbors (which ones do we affiliate with?).

Research has shown that something similar happens during neurodevelopment to increase risk for schizophrenia (see review by McGlashan & Hoffman, 2000). Neurons are produced in the inner layers of the brain and, during the second trimester, are transported outward to their destinations. But when something goes wrong with the transportation (cell migration) process, neurons do not arrive at the intended address. Typically, they stop just short of their destinations. Because neurons automatically reach out to establish connections with other neurons, they now form connections with their neighbors. But because these neurons are in the wrong location, they cannot set up optimal connections. What began as a minor problem in transportation becomes a major problem, and it is now more difficult for neurons to perform their main job, which is to communicate with other neurons and to process information.

Microscopic Studies of Brains

For a close look at neurons and their connections, we rely on microscopic examinations that can only be obtained upon autopsy. The neurons for persons with schizophrenia seem to be out of place and out of alignment. For example, some studies examined the arrangement of cells in an area of the brain called the hippocampus (discussed in chapter 5). Comparison subjects had neurons that were neatly aligned in the same orientation. But the neurons for schizophrenic individuals were in disarray, as if they had lost their sense of direction (Conrad, Abebe, Austin, Forsythe, & Scheibel, 1991; Kovelman & Scheibel, 1984).

Neurons cannot change their orientation once they are in position after migration; they essentially become "packed in" with other cells and have no room to move. So, it appears that cells in individuals with schizophrenia had not migrated correctly from the outset.

Other microscopic studies focused on the outer layer of the brain, called the cortex (literally, the "bark"), where most of the high-level information processing occurs. The cortex has a multilayered structure (much like the strata in a geological cross section) called "cytoarchitecture." Certain staining techniques used in identifying individual neurons have revealed a type of neural displacement in schizophrenia. There appear to be too few cells in the outermost layers of the brain (closer to the skull) and too many cells in the deeper layers (Arnold, Hyman, Van Hoesen, & Damasio, 1991; Jakob & Beckman, 1986). Figure 2.5 comes from one such study and depicts a cross section of the brain, with the outer layers at the top and the inner layers at the bottom. Each square on the figure represents a cell that was stained with an enzyme called NADPH. The cells from the patients are displaced inward; that is, they tend to be located in deeper layers of the brain when compared with the controls (Akbarian et al., 1993; Akbarian et al., 1996). The cortex develops in much the same manner that pioneers settled the Western frontier, with each wave of settlers passing the previous one and settling a little further west. Likewise, during cell migration, neurons move in an "inside-out" fashion, with each wave traveling past the previous wave before settling. Hence the inward displacement of cells has special meaning: It suggests that the neurons failed to migrate as far as they should have.

Even if neurons arrive at the wrong location, they still go to work setting up connections with other neurons. They do so by growing extensions, including both *dendrites* (similar to tree branches) to receive information and *axons* (similar to tree trunks) to send information (see figure 1 of the color insert). The connections with other neurons occur at *synapses*, areas of chemical communication between neurons. Initially the neurons generate plenty of dendrites and axons. But forming the right connections is not just a matter of growing more axons and

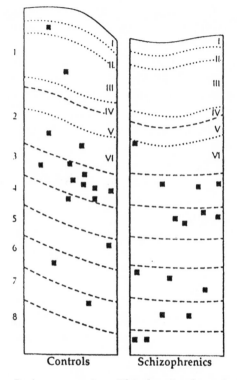

Figure 2.5 ■ *Brain cross sections. This drawing from the frontal region of a patient and a control, depicts the location of neurons that accept a certain type of stain (NADPH). The top of the figure is the cortical surface. There is a significant shift to the deeper (lower) levels in the brain of the patient. The roman numerals show the standard cortical layers, and numbers 1 through 8 indicate compartments segmented for this study. From Akbarian et al., 1993. Courtesy of the American Medical Association.*

dendrites and creating more synapses. It is also a matter of removing connections that are not necessary, a process known as "pruning," in which some of the dendrites and synapses disappear. Pruning a neuron is like pruning a tree—certain branches (dendrites) are cut so that the rest of the tree (neuron) is healthier. In the case of the neuron, only certain dendrites are selected for pruning, probably based on how communicative they were with other neurons.

The neuron's job is to process information, and from that point of view, too many neural connections are just as bad as too few. Imagine that you are trying out new phone systems. One system gives a clear signal, but it does not connect with all of your friends and family. It has too few connections. Another system connects to the people you want, but it also connects simultaneously to many strangers, so that you have to talk over several ongoing conversations. It has too many connections. You want a system that connects you with whom you want and no one else. That is what happens with neural connections when all goes well.

If neurons in schizophrenia do not arrive at their intended locations (perhaps due to inward displacement), it means they are communicating with the wrong neurons or with too few of the right ones. Normally, pruning is expected to increase the right connections and to eliminate the unnecessary connections. When problems in communication exist, the pruning is less directed and more haphazard. In effect, this is a vicious cycle, because when pruning runs amok it further disrupts processing of information (David, 1994; Hoffman & McGlashan, 1993). In support of the idea that pruning is abnormal in schizophrenia, certain layers of the cortex appear to be packed more densely in schizophrenic patients than in controls (Selemon, Rajkowska, & Goldman-Rakic, 1995). The overly dense packing is quite possibly a reflection of excessive pruning (e.g., fewer dendrites), which caused the neurons to squeeze together. Neurons in the brain are much like trees in a forest: Trees with small branches can grow closer together than trees with big branches.

Summarizing across studies, we can speculate that the neurons of patients fail to migrate normally to the outer layers of cortex, stopping short at the deeper cortical layers. This displacement is associated with a failure to make the right initial connections. In turn, these reduced connections apparently lead to abnormalities in pruning and to a denser packing of neurons. Most important, if the neurons are in the wrong location and/or overly pruned, their connections are not likely to be entirely correct. They have connections, but not the optimal ones.

> The data do not suggest that there are dead or missing cortical regions, or that some or many cortical regions are completely out of touch with each other (i.e., disconnected). Rather, they suggest that neuronal connections and circuits are to some degree anomalous and that cortical laminae and regions may be "dysconnected.". . . It is likely to translate into inefficient or "noisy" processing rather than no processing, into cortical communication that is "misinformed" rather than uninformed. (Weinberger & Lipska, 1995, pp. 89–90)

Indirect evidence has been mounting that schizophrenia involves reduced neural connectivity, but it has been hard to test this possibility in a direct manner. New techniques offer fairly direct support for reduced connectivity in schizophrenia. For example, it is possible to measure a substance called *synaptophysin,* which is a membrane protein and is critical for transmission of neurotransmitters at the synapse. Synaptophysin serves as a measure of neural connections, with higher levels indicating more synapses and therefore more neural connections. Consistent with reduced connectivity, figure 2 of the color insert shows that a brain of a schizophrenic patient contains less synaptophysin than one from a comparison subject (Glantz & Lewis, 1997). From this, and from studies of neurocognition mentioned in chapter 4 and neuroimaging in chapter 5, we are beginning to assemble a picture of schizophrenia as a disorder primarily of disconnection. The illness starts with disconnection at the neural level and leads to disconnection at the interpersonal level.

The microscopic studies described above were done on autopsy and were obviously limited because we cannot collect further data about the symptoms, behaviors, and performance of the individuals. Newer techniques, however, are emerging that can be used *in vivo* (with living people) to tell us about the integrity of the neuron components responsible for communication with other neurons. For example, one type of neuroimaging called diffusion tensor imaging (discussed later in chapter 5) revealed that the brains of schizophrenic individuals had less developed communication tracts (such as axons) compared with controls (Lim et al., 1999). This technique provides rather strong support for the idea of reduced connectivity in the brains of schizophrenic patients.

Risk versus Onset of Illness

As the importance of early neurodevelopmental factors for schizophrenia has become well established, terms that were once simple have become complicated. *Onset* is one such term. The onset of schizophrenia is not the start of the disease; it is the end product of predisposition mixed with risk factors. But if onset of illness is the result of a long and circuitous process, we are stuck with a perplexing puzzle. Why do the overt symptoms begin so much later than the underlying neural events? We have signs of schizophrenia that start earlier than the symptoms (such as those seen in home movies). Nonetheless, the time frame for the more dramatic symptoms is much delayed. We do not have a complete answer to this question, but we have some good leads. Daniel Weinberger (1987, 1995) has speculated that the neural disruption is present very early, but the effects are not seen because the disruption involves brain regions that are not very active until the second or third decade of life. A simple example will make this clear. For centuries, parents have wondered if there is something wrong with the brains of their adolescent children. And now we know there is—their *bodies* mature faster than their *brains*, which develop in an uneven fashion, with different rates of maturation for different regions. One of the areas of greatest interest for schizophrenia is the prefrontal cortex, an area not fully mature until late adolescence. A disruption in the prefrontal region (perhaps due to abnormal cell migration) in the second trimester may not have appreciable effects until the prefrontal cortex is fully developed and called upon to perform cognitive operations some two decades later. It is like having a damaged file in your computer—you only know there is a problem when you try to use the file. Otherwise, the problem lies unnoticed.

An alternative has been offered by Elaine Walker and colleagues. They suggested that the time delay between the accumulation of risk factors and the onset of symptoms could involve an interaction between neurotransmitters (the chemical messengers in the brain) and hormones that interact with neurotransmitters. Adolescence is frequently a time of life changes, demands for complex problem solving, and increased stress. Perhaps stress at this time of life increases the release of cortisol, a stress-related hormone, which in turn increases the activity of the neurotransmitter dopamine. Such an increase in dopamine activity could contribute to the onset of symptoms (Walker & DiForio, 1997).

Neurodevelopmental versus Progressive Disorder

This chapter has focused on neurodevelopmental factors for schizophrenia. For most of the twentieth century, however, the focus of research was on the later, not the earlier, part of the life span. Schizophrenia was seen as a progressively deteriorating disease, as emphasized in the early descriptions by Kraepelin. In fact, it was this downward course that Kraepelin claimed differentiated schizophrenia from mood disorders such as manic depressive illness.

Long-standing notions of schizophrenia as a progressive illness were challenged for two reasons. First, as mentioned in previous sections, evidence suggested that early, particularly prenatal, factors influence risk for schizophrenia. Second, on close inspection, schizophrenia did not look much like a progressive illness. In comparison to disorders such as Alzheimer's Disease, schizophrenia does not have an obvious downward course. The symptoms of schizophrenia do not necessarily worsen with time (which would be expected from a deteriorating condition). Instead, clinical symptoms generally mellow with age.

The evidence that schizophrenia is a *developmental* illness is overwhelming for reasons mentioned in this chapter including (1) risk for illness can be influenced by very early (e.g., prenatal) events, (2) adult individuals with schizophrenia carry signs of developmental problems (e.g., minor physical anomalies), and (3) the brains of people with schizophrenia carry telltale markers of aberrant neurodevelopment. The course of illness also suggests a developmental component. For example, pre-schizophrenic children often have subtle behavioral, emotional, and motoric abnormalities starting at a young age, indicating problems in development.

On the other hand, a strong argument can be made that schizophrenia is also *progressive* because, based on neuroimaging studies, it appears that some brain changes, such as shrinkage, occur even after the onset of illness (DeLisi et al., 1997; Gur et al., 1998; Rapoport et al., 1999). If the disorder were only developmental, the brain would develop more slowly and fail to reach its maximum size. Instead, it appears to grow to its full size and then decrease slightly, indicating a progressive process. Also, to get a diagnosis of schizophrenia, there must be a loss of social functioning from a previous level, suggesting a progressive component.

Resolving these debates will require reframing the question. It is not a matter of whether schizophrenia is a developmental *or* a deteriorating disorder; the illness has features of both. Two types of processes (neurodevelopmental and progressive) may be present in schizophrenia, which would make it a "progressive neurodevelopmental" disorder (McGlashan & Hoffman, 2000; Woods, 1998). Perhaps an aberrant process disrupts neural events during the prenatal period, but the disruption does not stop at the end of this period. Instead the offending process continues for a couple of decades. For example, excessive pruning of dendrites and axons may start early in life, during the prenatal period, and may continue during childhood and adolescence. The effects of this excessive pruning may be subtle or even unnoticed during early childhood. But at some point a threshold is crossed (e.g., too many dendrites are trimmed so that the effects are no longer subtle) and clinical symptoms begin. Hence schizophrenia may be considered a neurodevelopmental disorder because the neural disruptions begin in the prenatal period, and a progressive disorder because they continue well beyond that time.

Chapter Three

The Genetics of Schizophrenia

Looking In The Blood

Mark Twain once quipped that giving up smoking "is the easiest thing. . . . I've done it a thousand times." Likewise, finding the gene for schizophrenia must be the easiest thing—apparently we've done it a thousand times. Just look how often newspapers announce the discovery.

Perhaps the attraction of the news story lies in the juxtaposition of a very mysterious illness with a seemingly hard scientific finding. But claims about locating the gene for schizophrenia tend to be overstated and misleading. Indeed, the statements from genetic researchers are typically crafted with caution; consequently, they are dull and get buried deep in the article. What makes the claims overstated? For starters, very few researchers believe that schizophrenia will be explained by a single gene. Instead, it is considered to be "genetically complex," meaning that the illness almost certainly involves the interactions of a large number of genes. In addition, finding evidence of genetic involvement or even genetic linkage is one thing, but finding "the gene" for schizophrenia is quite another.

Schizophrenia is undoubtably a genetic disorder (Gottesman, 1991; Kendler & Diehl, 1993). In the not-so-distant past, it was possible to have an honest difference of opinion about this point, but not anymore. Estimates of the heritability of schizophrenia range from 74 percent to almost 90 percent (McGue, Gottesman, & Rao, 1983; McGuffin, Asherson, Owen, & Farmer, 1994). Hence the most important factors for the development of schizophrenia are conveyed through genetics.

Schizophrenia, however, is not a standard, simple genetic disorder. When people think about genetic diseases, they often think about disorders such as Huntington's Disease or cystic fibrosis. These disorders involve one major gene and are unusual in their genetic simplicity. Schizophrenia is one of many other disorders (along with coronary artery disease and hypertension) that are considered "complex" genetic disorders involving the actions and interactions of multiple genes.

Research on the genetics of schizophrenia has proceeded in two distinctly different ways. For several decades, studies of "classical" genetics dominated. These studies looked at families, twins, and adoptees to tease apart genetic influences. These studies were conducted on the strength of excellent national records and old-fashioned psychiatric interviews. Not one drop of blood was drawn, nor one chromosome examined. Nonetheless, these studies established that schizophrenia was largely, though not entirely, genetic.

Subsequent studies have taken advantage of the current developments in molecular genetics: scientists draw a small amount of blood from participants, extract the genetic material, and dismantle strands of DNA as if they were tiny Lego toys. These molecular approaches have considerable promise and as we will see, also present formidable challenges.

Classical Approaches

Family Studies

There used to be a bumper sticker that read, "Mental illness is hereditary. You catch it from your kids." Families are often painfully aware of the genetic risk that runs in families. In the following quote, a mother expresses her feelings of concern, and ultimate helplessness, as she confronts the results of increased risk of schizophrenia in her offspring:

When I married and had children, I tried to compensate with good parenting skills for any predisposition toward mental illness they might have inherited from their grandfather. Ironically, we also found mental illness in my husband's family later on. Moreover, childhood emotional trauma or skewed family relationships do not cause schizophrenia. When three of our eight children developed schizophrenia, it was probably inevitable. (Malloy, 1998, p. 495)

The idea that mental illness is a family affair is found worldwide. This view often has unforeseen consequences, including the possibility that the stigma will be shared by the immediate family. Consider the situation in India where there is substantial stigma associated with mental illness, and marriages are frequently arranged. A survey conducted in Chandigarh India asked whether people agreed with the following statement: "We should make it clear to our children that they should not select a marriage partner who has been treated for mental illness in the past." The question was presented to both medical and psychiatric patients. A large number (about 70 percent) of the medical patients agreed with the statement. Perhaps even more revealing was that 75 percent of the *psychiatric* patients also agreed with the statement (Malhotra, Inam, & Chopra, 1981). In India, this deep-seated reaction to mental illness is a major obstacle to finding a suitable mate for someone with a history of mental illness. To make matters worse, an illness like schizophrenia in an older sibling can present an obstacle to arranging a marriage for a younger sibling. This has direct public health implications because family members are eager to keep any mental illness in the family out of the public eye; the result is that treatment for a family member is often delayed until the disorder is far advanced.

Schizophrenia does indeed run in families, not with certainty for any one person but with a rate higher than would be expected. Family studies show that about 8 percent of siblings and 5 percent of parents of a schizophrenic individual will have schizophrenia, compared to roughly 1 percent in the general population (Holzman & Matthysse, 1990). The rates in parents are lower than siblings because many people with schizophrenia (especially men) do not become parents. Children of schizophrenic individuals have about a 12 percent chance of developing schizophrenia.

If family members are at increased risk for schizophrenia, are they also at increased risk for other psychiatric disorders? As it turns out, relatives are at risk for some schizophrenia-related conditions (Kendler & Diehl, 1993). For example, rates of Schizotypal Personality Disorder (characterized by odd and eccentric behavior) and Paranoid Personality Disorder (characterized by suspicious behavior) are increased. These are not psychotic disorders; instead, they are long-standing personality traits that are similar to, but milder than, the symptoms of schizophrenia. Family members also have increased rates for other psychotic disorders such as Schizoaffective Disorder (described in chapter 1). But the rates for family members are *not* increased for most other psychiatric disorders, including depression, anxiety, and alcoholism. Overall, family studies indicate that relatives of an individual with schizophrenia have increased risks for a "spectrum" of illnesses similar to schizophrenia, but not for mental illness in general.

Schizophrenia may run in families, but not all traits that run in families are genetic. Drinking red wine runs in Italian families, but it takes considerable mental acrobatics to attribute this behavior to anything other than environmental influences. In searching for explanations of this behavior we do not feel compelled to invoke a red-wine-drinking gene that lurks in the Italian blood. We have a much simpler explanation: If you are raised with red wine at dinner, odds are good that you will maintain this custom when you get older. Because of the interpretive limitation of family studies, the classical genetics of schizophrenia have relied heavily on twin and adoption studies.

Twin Studies

Nature has been kind to geneticists by providing two types of twins, identical and fraternal. Identical twins come from the same zygote (fertilized egg) and are called monozygotic (MZ) twins. Fraternal twins come from two different zygotes and are called dizygotic (DZ) twins. MZ twins share 100 percent of their genes, whereas DZ twins share 50 percent of their genes, the same as any two siblings. By comparing the rates of disorders in these two sets of twins, we can get a handle on whether there is a genetic component. Suppose we have a disease that is entirely genetic. If one MZ twin has the disease, the other should also have it. We say that the rate of *concordance* (correspondence) should be 100 percent. The rate of concordance for DZ twins should be much lower—the same as whatever the rate is for siblings. Now suppose that a disease is entirely due to environmental factors. In this case, the concordance rates for MZ and DZ twins should be about the same. The fact that MZ twins share more of their genes than do DZ twins becomes irrelevant if the malady is caused by environment. In this way, comparisons of MZ and DZ twins can answer questions in schizophrenia—the logic being that if the concordance rates for MZ twins are higher than those for DZ twins, then there has to be a genetic component.

There are many twin studies in schizophrenia; the concordance rates vary somewhat, but the rates for MZ twins are always higher than for DZ twins. A reasonable estimate is provided by Irving Gottesman, who calculated that the concordance rates across studies are 48 percent for MZ twins compared with 17 percent for DZ twins (Gottesman, 1991). The nearly three-fold difference in concordance is hard to explain any way other than genetics.

What about MZ twins raised apart? At first glance, this seems like a great way to assess the genetics of schizophrenia. Reports of non-schizophrenic MZ twins raised apart (the most famous ones come from scientists at the University of Minnesota) have revealed striking patterns of heritability for specific mental abilities, personality, and interests (Bouchard, Lykken, McGue, Segal, & Tellegen, 1990). There are bewildering anecdotes of twins reared apart making similar choices, such as both having a wife or a pet of the same name. But this kind of study cannot readily be done with schizophrenia since the necessary conditions occur so rarely. The chance of this situation arising depends on one fairly rare event (MZ twins) multiplied by another relatively uncommon event (having schizophrenia) multiplied by one exceedingly rare event (MZ twins separated and reared apart). Only about a dozen cases have been reported in the worldwide literature. The concordance for these cases is conservatively estimated at 58 percent—even higher than the estimate of 48 percent for MZ twins raised together (Gottesman & Shields, 1982).

One detailed example of MZ twins raised apart is provided by Gottesman and Shields (1982), who encountered the men while conducting a twin study in London.

> The twins, referred to as Herbert and Nick, were born in 1934 to a 19-year-old half-Chinese woman. The father was a pinball machine repairman who impregnated the young woman and was not seen by her again. The twins were separated at birth and raised in a different series of foster homes. During World War II, they were united for less than a year at the time of the evacuation of London. Following the war, Herbert went to live with his maternal grandmother. She, however, did not want to raise Nick, so she gave him to a 41-year-old married and childless woman. One year later, at 42, the woman became pregnant.
>
> Family life for Herbert in the grandmother's family was described as distant, whereas the family life for Nick in his adopted family with the younger step-sibling was described as caring and warm. The twins were aware of each other's existence, but had only rare contact as they were growing up. With such separate lives, it is hard to explain their similar behavior during adolescence: both were bed wetters until early teens; both set fires; and both were thieves. Nor can we fully explain the similar neurocognitive assessments in the army: both were considered to be illiterate, both had below-average IQ's, both served honorably, and both were assigned menial jobs. After the army, both worked as delivery boys until the

age of 22. At that time, both were experiencing increasing delusional thoughts (mainly persecutory for Herbert, mainly grandiose for Nick). Most astonishing is that Herbert and Nick were hospitalized for the first time within three days of each other. They remained in separate psychiatric hospitals for most of the next 20 years.

A glass half full is, by necessity, also half empty. The 48 percent concordance for MZ twins means that an MZ co-twin of an ill twin does *not* develop schizophrenia about half of the time. How can we explain this? If schizophrenia were entirely genetic, the chances should be 100 percent. First of all, schizophrenia has a substantial genetic component, but it is not entirely a genetic disorder. Also, as stated earlier, schizophrenia is a disorder of risks or predisposition. What one inherits is the risk for schizophrenia, not the certainty of it. There are no guarantees that any one person will develop schizophrenia, even if they are predisposed.

A set of MZ twins begins life with about the same predisposition to schizophrenia. But their environments differ, starting in the womb. As the twins grow older they will encounter different risk factors and protectors. What decides if one vulnerable twin develops schizophrenia and the other does not? In the case of MZ twins discordant for schizophrenia, it has much to do with something that is rarely mentioned and never taken seriously in behavioral science—*luck*. When one twin develops schizophrenia and the identical co-twin does not, it may be like the Albert King blues classic says, that if it wasn't for bad luck they would have no luck at all. An unequal distribution of nutrients in the womb, a high fever as an infant, a different choice of activities leading to a different circle of friends, a head injury playing baseball, an automobile accident, different levels of emotional support from friends and family—all of these might make the difference in outcome for an individual who is predisposed. The 48 percent concordance for MZ twins that share the same genes and are raised by the same parents is a reminder that one inherits predisposition only, and differences in outcome are due to factors beyond genetics, including some within the individual's control (such as heavy drug use, or driving recklessly) but many that are not (e.g., differential nutrients in the womb).

Adoption Studies

Adoption studies are probably the best way to separate and examine genetic and environmental factors. Many of the adoption studies were conducted in Nordic countries, the main reason being that countries like Finland, Denmark, Sweden, and Norway have superb national records for adoptions and psychiatric hospitalizations, which made it relatively easy to locate individuals in national registries for studies of mental illness. Unlike the United States, these countries also have populations that are geographically stable, meaning that people tend to live their entire lives in one region. An adoption study can start with the mother or with the adoptee. If we start with the mothers, then the question is whether the rates of schizophrenia are unusually high in the adopted-away offspring of mothers who had schizophrenia. This approach needs two groups of mothers who give up children for adoption at an early age—one group with schizophrenia and a comparison group that does not have a psychiatric disorder. This type of investigation can be done retrospectively if the records are very good. Such studies have shown that adoptees born to mothers with schizophrenia have higher rates of schizophrenia themselves, even though they are not raised with their biological mothers (Heston, 1966; Rosenthal, Wender, Kety, Welner, & Schulsinger, 1971).

Instead of starting with the mother, we can start with two groups of adoptees—one group with schizophrenia and a comparison group without. Each group of adoptees has two sets of relatives, biological and adoptive. If schizophrenia is a primarily genetic disorder, one group of relatives, the *biological* relatives of the schizophrenic adoptees, should have higher rates of schizophrenia. If schizophrenia is largely environmental, then the *adopted* relatives of the schizophrenic adoptees should have higher rates. And if the disorder appears randomly, then all four sets of relatives should have roughly the same rates. In fact, the biological relatives of the schizophrenic adoptees have higher rates of schizophrenia. In a nationwide study in Denmark, 5 percent of the biological relatives of schizophrenic adoptees had schizophrenia themselves, but the rates were all well under 1 percent for the three remaining groups of relatives (Kety et al., 1994). Again, it is hard to explain this type of result through any mechanism other than genetics.

A third way to conduct an adoption study is to look at children with non-schizophrenic mothers who were adopted into families in which one of the parents developed schizophrenia. Presumably, to qualify for the adoption, the parents did not show signs of schizophrenia at the time of the adoption. In this case you have a child who probably does not have a predisposition to schizophrenia but is being reared by a parent with schizophrenia. Do these children have higher rates of schizophrenia than a comparison group of adoptees who were adopted by parents without psychiatric problems? The answer is no—the rates of schizophrenia-related symptoms are about the same. Schizophrenia may run in families, but we do not "catch" it just by living with our parents.

What if someone had a high risk for schizophrenia from birth and was raised by schizophrenic parents. Would that make a difference? In Northern Finland, a team of investigators headed by Pekka Tienari (1991) has cleverly looked at the relationship of children's risk for schizophrenia to their rearing environment. They used national records from the entire country to identify two groups of adoptees. One group had biological mothers with schizophrenia; the comparison group of adoptees had biological mothers without psychosis. So far, this approach sounds familiar. But the investigators took their research one step forward. They conducted lengthy interviews with the adopting families and classified them as healthy or disturbed. The ratings were based mainly on patterns of interactions among family members. Families rated as "disturbed" did not necessarily have any members with psychosis, but they did have problematic patterns of communication and behavior, unresolved conflicts, and sometimes individuals who adopted inappropriate family roles. The researchers reasoned that the offspring of a schizophrenic parent may be very sensitive to the influences of his or her environment. A healthy family may be protective for the child, whereas a disturbed family environment may be noxious. Indeed, researchers found that the adoptees who had mothers with schizophrenia had higher rates of psychosis and other forms of mental illness than did the comparison group—but only when reared in families that were considered disturbed. In the families rated as healthy, there were no differences. The conclusion is inescapable: that the predisposition for schizophrenia is largely genetic, but whether or not that predisposition blossoms into schizophrenia depends on many nongenetic factors.

Shotguns and Lasers: Studies of Molecular Genetics

In contrast to the studies of classical genetics, which have little to do with DNA per se, studies of molecular genetics move in for a closer look (Burmeister, 1999; Hyman, 1999). All of our genetic material is housed in the double helix of DNA. The strands of DNA are assembled into our 23 chromosomes. Each DNA strand is made up of many (about 3 billion) building blocks called nucleotide bases, or base pairs (because there are two strands of DNA). A sequence of these bases forms a gene. In essence, a gene is a location on the DNA that contains a sequence of bases that enables the cell to make a certain protein. Humans have about 80,000 to 100,000 genes. Genes come in different forms, or versions, called alleles. In order for these alleles (gene variations) to have a consequence for the individual, they must alter something in the way the protein is produced. For example, if a gene contains the code for a certain protein involved in the synthesis of a substance in the brain, different alleles of that gene might produce more or less of that protein, produce the protein at the wrong time, or not produce it at all.

We can already see how complicated matters become when we start looking for a schizophrenia gene. A schizophrenia-relevant gene may have many alleles, but only one or two of these alleles might increase the risk for schizophrenia. For this reason, it is technically incorrect to say that we are looking for a "gene" for schizophrenia. We are looking for a particular version of a gene (an allele) that contributes to risk for the disorder.

In molecular genetics, scientists usually select one of two general approaches. One approach (linkage studies) seeks the connection between a region on a chromosome and the disorder. Since we do not exactly know where to look on the chromosome, this approach can be compared to shooting a shotgun and then looking around to see what we hit. The other approach (association studies) first searches for a particular gene since the product of this gene (its protein) is considered relevant to the disorder. This method is more like using a laser beam and requires a rather clear idea of what one is looking for.

Shotguns: Linkage Studies

Linkage studies take a "shotgun" approach and look at the entire genome to see if there is a link between a certain region of a chromosome and the disorder. Linkage studies require "markers" that indicate a certain location on a chromosome. To develop genetic markers, we rely on proteins called restriction enzymes that act like microscopic scalpels. They run around the DNA; whenever they see a particular base pair sequence, they cleave it. Different alleles for a gene often have a different number of base pairs that produce variable lengths of the cleaved DNA segments. These length differences of the alleles can be measured with sensitive laboratory methods. All this cleaving and measuring can be used to mark certain locations on the DNA. These studies collect DNA from a family that has several members with schizophrenia, as well as many members who are not ill. Scientists compare the marker alleles in the affected members to the unaffected members. Demonstrating that the affected members have the same marker allele and the non-ill members do not, shows genetic linkage for the disease.

But the marker allele, even if it occurs with affected members, probably has nothing to do with schizophrenia—it just marks a location. Linkage analyses make a simple and safe assumption: that if affected members share the same markers, the relevant alleles for schizophrenia cannot be far away. The basis for this assumption is that we inherit our DNA in chunks. When our parents passed on their DNA to us, they did so in pieces of a chromosome. It was not like mom and dad took turns giving us one DNA base at a time; they gave us lengthy strands. Combining the strands of DNA from parents to make the DNA of the offspring is like shuffling a deck of cards, but not doing a very thorough job. Certain card sequences will remain in the shuffled deck. Nature shuffled the DNA of our parents with all the care of a 10-year-old eager for her next hand of cards; and this is a good thing for studies of genetics. It means that if the affected members of a family have the same marker alleles, the schizophrenia-relevant alleles should be in the same neighborhood of the chromosome because there is a good chance the alleles got transferred from parent to offspring in the same chunk of DNA.

Several locations have already been linked to schizophrenia, including regions of chromosomes 5, 6, 8, 10, 13, and 22 (Pulver, 2000). Successful linkage studies reveal a region of DNA, not an individual gene. Analogously, this is like knowing only the city where a house is located versus knowing the street address for a house. As Margit Burmeister has written, "Finding linkage only means we have a reasonable likelihood of knowing where on a chromosome to look for a gene!" (1999, p. 526).

Lasers: Association Studies

It is important to remember that linkage studies yield genetic markers and chromosomal regions of interest, but they do not by themselves tell us much about the causes of the disorder. Linkage studies do not require any particular knowledge about the causes of the disease. You perform linkage studies in roughly the same way, whether you're looking at the genetics of schizophrenia, alcoholism, or double chins. In contrast, association studies have a narrow, laserlike focus. These studies begin with a particular gene in mind—one that is considered relevant to the disorder. Let's consider a fanciful analogy. Suppose we have good reason to believe that schizophrenia is caused by abnormalities in a substance secreted from the big toe. If we know something about this substance, it will help us know where to look on the genome. The game plan would be first to identify a gene responsible for that substance—for example, one that contains the code for a protein used in synthesizing the substance. Next we would compare this gene in patients and a control group. If the two groups have different alleles of this gene, then we know we were right—it was the big toe after all.

This type of approach is *thoughtful*—you first need to know the biochemical process that is relevant for the disease. But it is not that simple. For one, we have a rough draft only of the human genome, not a detailed map. We may have a hunch about which substance is aberrant in schizophrenia and still have no idea where it is coded on the genome. The encouraging news is that the details are being filled in for the entire human genome. In landmark projects originating from both public and private sectors, researchers around the world are plodding through the genome, fleshing out specifics at an impressive rate. This achievement is truly remarkable. Working drafts are already available, and soon we will know where genes of interest are located. This will be an essential step, but association genetic studies for schizophrenia will still be difficult after the task is completed.

Even if we target a single substance that is important for schizophrenia, we will not be looking for a single gene. For years the substances of greatest interest for schizophrenia have been neurotransmitters, the chemical messengers in the brain. Typically, the production of a neurotransmitter takes many steps—a series of precursor substances must be successively converted into the neurotransmitter. Various proteins that are coded by the genes play multiple roles in this process: they are both the precursors and the enzymes that regulate each step in the conversion process. So, even if we are interested in one neurotransmitter, there might be a dozen or more genes (proteins) directly involved, and many more with indirect influence. We have not even begun to talk about the receptors for the neurotransmitters (where they bind to the neuron), which are comprised of yet another batch of proteins.

Keep in mind that the association approach is only as good as our hunch. The substance we think is relevant today for schizophrenia may not necessarily be the one we will think is relevant tomorrow. We have been surprised before and will be surprised again. We could invest years studying the genetic code that regulates the secretion from the big toe only to learn the folly of our ways and find out that it was the secretion from the thumb all along. This warning strikes close to home because schizophrenia has long centered on one particular neurotransmitter, dopamine. In recent years, as new findings come to light and new medications are introduced, the focus has expanded considerably. Other neurotransmitter systems, including serotonin, GABA, acetylcholine, and glutamate, are actively being investigated.

A Phenotype by Any Other Name

The biggest problem we face in the genetics of schizophrenia concerns the *phenotype*, not the *genotype*. The genotype is at the level of DNA base pairs; it is the genetic code itself. The phenotype is observable; it is a feature that can be traced back to the protein produced by a particular gene. The genotype for eye color is embedded deep in your DNA; your baby blues are the phenotype. For the genetics of schizophrenia, the phenotype has been a diagnosis of schizophrenia based on the criteria from the *DSM*. It all sounds so logical, and we have been reliably diagnosing the disorder for decades. So, what's the problem? Consider a statement by the current director of the United States National Institute of Mental Health (NIMH):

> Compounding the difficulties in psychiatry is the problem of defining phenotypes; indeed for mental disorders this may be the most difficult problem of all. While the ... *DSM-IV* is a useful tool for communication, it would be foolhardy to think that its criteria select anything that maps onto the genome. (Hyman, 1999, p. 519)

Blasphemy? It sounds odd to say that our search for the genetics of schizophrenia has nothing to do with the diagnosis of clinical schizophrenia. This is not a minority opinion, however. Not only is it hard to decide on a reasonable phenotype, it is also extremely difficult to measure some phenotypes. Leading experts in the genetics of schizophrenia wrote, "Simply measuring the phenotype is without doubt the hardest task in the linkage analysis" (Freedman, Adler, & Leonard, 1999, p. 555).

This problem for genetic studies could not be more fundamental—we are not sure what to call schizophrenia. Do we view schizophrenia as a collection of psychotic symptoms, or as a collection of risks and predispositions? The sobering truth is that the *technological* advances in genetics have outpaced the *conceptual* advances. The impressive techniques for slicing and dicing strands of DNA and mapping the human genome step by step are not helpful if we are unsure what we mean by schizophrenia. This is part of the paradox introduced in the first chapter: Schizophrenia is a psychotic disorder, but it is not primarily a disorder of psychotic symptoms. Using clinical schizophrenia as the phenotype for genetic studies has proved terribly problematic.

To understand why this is a problem, consider a whimsical example. Imagine that, despite the obvious societal taboos, an IBM PC computer elopes with an Apple computer. This inter-platform union results in three adorable little laptop computers. One is an IBM and one is an Apple; both are pure and simple. The third offspring is more complex—it looks like, and mainly functions like, an IBM. But a close inspection of its circuitry reveals that its processing chip was originally configured for an Apple. In essence, this little machine was *predisposed* to be an Apple, but it did not become one. Now, suppose that this cyber-family is participating in a study of the genetics of Apple computers. Which members are considered to be Apples? Mama Apple and baby Apple, certainly. What about our little hybrid? It should be counted as well. For genetic studies of schizophrenia, one's predisposition (the genotype) is more important than what one eventually becomes (the phenotype).

Now for a more realistic example, take a look at figure 3.1. This figure uses a standard format to represent two parents and four offspring. Two of the offspring have clinical schizophrenia (shown in black). Neither parent has schizophrenia; so where did the disorder come from in the offspring? The answer becomes clear when we consider an *alternative* phenotype. An alternative

phenotype is one that does not rely on the diagnosis of schizophrenia, or even on traditional clinical symptoms. Alternative
phenotypes are indications that a schizophrenia-relevant gene is
present, and they can include neurocognitive deficits or electrophysiological abnormalities.

The rationale for using alternative phenotypes stems from a
central assumption about the genetics of schizophrenia:
Schizophrenia almost certainly involves more than one gene. For
the sake of argument, let's say there are 17 main schizophrenia-
relevant genes (this example is, of course, vastly simplified and
ignores the fact there can be genes of major and minor effects).
Recall that the genes provide the predisposition for schizophrenia, but not the assurance that one will develop the illness. Each
of these schizophrenia-relevant genes brings about changes in
proteins (e.g., the schizophrenia-relevant allele makes too much
or too little of the protein). In turn, each of the 17 specific
proteins bring about changes in a specific function. How would
we see the actions of these genes? Perhaps with neurocognitive or
electrophysiological tasks like those discussed in the next chapter (such as measures of attention or perception). Abnormalities
on these types of tasks can serve as an alternative phenotype.

The problem of limiting ourselves to one clinically based
phenotype (the diagnosis of clinical schizophrenia) is that it may,
or may not, be present, even when a person has a schizophrenia-
relevant genes. In contrast, the alternative phenotype is expected
to be present whenever the gene is; it is more tightly linked to the
genotype. Use of these alternative phenotypes should lead us
more directly to the relevant gene, and they help us to understand pedigrees, like those in figure 3.1. In this figure, individuals
who have the alternative phenotype are marked "AP." Now we can
see clearly that one parent and one of the offspring had the alternative phenotype, but did not have the disorder. By using alternative phenotypes, it becomes easier to see where the risk came
from and who among the offspring has it. It is also much easier to
link the genotype to the alternative phenotype.

A closely related problem with using clinical schizophrenia as
the phenotype for genetic studies is simple arithmetic; schizo-

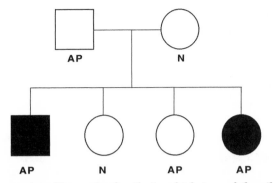

Figure 3.1 ■ *A pedigree of a family in which two of the siblings are affected with clinical schizophrenia (shown in black). Family members with the Alternate Phenotype are labeled AP. Males are depicted with squares; females with circles. From Freedman et al., 1999.*

phrenia is not very common, even when it runs in families. The analysis and interpretation of genetic studies requires a very large number of individuals with the disorder. As long as we limit ourselves to clinical schizophrenia, the relatively small numbers will erode any confidence in the findings. Such studies are said to lack sufficient "power," meaning that there are not enough subjects to draw firm conclusions. By using alternative phenotypes, we can dramatically increase the power of our studies because a much larger number of individuals may have one or more alternative phenotypes, compared to the number with clinical schizophrenia.

Another good reason to study alternative phenotypes is that they can give useful clues about underlying neurobiology. As discussed in the next chapter, an abnormality in perception might make a good alternative phenotype. To learn more about this abnormality, we might administer a perception task in a brain scanner, or administer the task to animals. Either way, we can gather information on the neural circuits for that task. In the process, we learn something about the biology as well as the genetics of schizophrenia. Using several alternative phenotypes in a convergent fashion is especially promising because we can look for areas of overlap. This approach, defined below, was predicted several years ago:

> As in navigation, fixing on several landmarks helps to triangulate one's position, so in the search for causes the attempt to make sense of divergent manifestations may point us toward an etiological process. A cell type in the brain common to the several manifestations; a shared neurotransmitter; a common developmental epoch; vascular supply from the same arterial bed. . . . Finding other traits associated with the gene for schizophrenia might do more than facilitate linkage analysis; it might give us clues about etiology. (Holzman & Matthysse, 1990, p. 285)

In the next chapter, we will describe several promising candidates for alternative phenotypes, including deficits in neurocognition and electrophysiology (attention, perception, sensory gating, eye tracking) that seem to reflect predisposition to schizophrenia. Robert Freedman and his colleagues successfully used a measure of sensory gating (P50 auditory evoked potential) as an alternative phenotype (Freedman et al., 1997). In this sensory gating procedure, a subject hears two clicks in rapid succession. Normally, the brain response to the second click is smaller than to the first. Schizophrenic patients show deficits on this procedure, meaning that they do not show as much of a reduction in brain response to the second click compared with controls. Using sensory gating as an alternative phenotype in a genetic linkage study not only provided more statistical "power," the procedure also provided clues about where to look on the genome. The neurobiology of the P50 procedure is reasonably established and it involves the nicotinic receptor (the same one occupied by nicotine from cigarettes). This knowledge about the biology of the alternative phenotype helped to focus the search of the research team as they sought out a gene for the nicotine receptor. Because of the increased power with an alternative phenotype, and because they had a hunch on where to look on the genome, this group showed strong linkage when sensory gating was used as an (alternative) phenotype. Using clinical schizophrenia as a phenotype did not provide enough power to make any firm interpretations.

In summary, the genetics of schizophrenia has gone through two phases. The first phase of classical genetics employed family, twin, and adoption studies to demonstrate that schizophrenia has a substantial genetic component. The studies also showed that one inherits only predisposition to illness, and that nongenetic factors can influence whether an individual actually develops the disorder. Although this phase of research convincingly showed genetic involvement in schizophrenia, it did not help to isolate relevant genes. The second phase is one of molecular genetics. Recent advances in genetics are being applied to schizophrenia, but the process so far has been challenging and frustrating, characterized by some successes, and numerous failures to replicate findings of linkages. The solution appears to require a new approach: The genetics of schizophrenia will be uncovered if we can let go of the clinical disorder itself and select an alternative phenotype more tightly liked to the genotype. Paradoxically, to make meaningful advances, the genetics of schizophrenia will probably require a phenotype other than schizophrenia.

Chapter Four

Neurocognitive Deficits

Neurocognitive deficits in schizophrenia cover a broad range, including difficulties with perception, attention, memory, problem solving, and some aspects of language, as well as deficits in aspects of social and interpersonal interactions. In this chapter, we will survey some of the tests that are used to assess neurocognitive functioning in schizophrenia. We will also consider whether neurocognitive deficits are central to schizophrenia. The question of "centrality" to schizophrenia is key, but the answer is slightly counterintuitive.

To illustrate the centrality issue, let's consider a whimsical example: Imagine that we want to know whether schizophrenic patients show deficits when playing Pin the Tail on the Donkey. To explore this possibility, we administer a "test" to two groups of subjects: schizophrenic patients and normal controls. Pin the Tail on the Donkey, in case you missed this part of growing up, involves several steps, including looking at a poster of a donkey that is hanging on a wall, getting a plastic "tail" that will stick to the poster, becoming blindfolded, being spun around like a top, and then serving as a source of amusement when you try to stick the tail in the right location on the picture. Scoring is based on how close you place the tail to the optimal location (i.e., the donkey's behind).

After conducting our tail-pinning experiment, we find that schizophrenic patients, on average, do not tail pin as well as normal controls. The data are irrefutable; the conclusion is inescapable: Patients have a "tail-pinning deficit." We write up the results, publish them, and, before we know it, everyone is complaining about the study. Why?

One disgruntled group of cognitive psychologists wastes no time in telling us that Pin the Tail on the Donkey is a "multidimensional" test—that is, it has many components and therefore a lot of different reasons for poor performance. Doing well on this test requires one to form an image of the wall and poster (visual memory), maintain orientation to the wall during spinning (integration of vestibular and spatial organizational skills), estimate the distance to the wall (integration of depth perception with gross visual imagery skills), estimate distance as one walks to the wall (integration of proprioceptive information), estimate the location of the donkey's behind (fine visual imagery and memory), and then place the tail where you intend (planning and execution of smooth graded movement). A failure in any one of these abilities could account for the tail-pinning deficit. Cognitive psychologists pointedly declare that, we may know that patients have a deficit, but we do not understand what causes it.

Clinicians who work directly with schizophrenia (e.g., psychiatrists, social workers, case managers) are no happier with the study, but for a different reason. Unlike cognitive psychologists who are unimpressed with the study because they do not understand the meaning of the results, clinicians are unimpressed with the study because they think they understand the results too well. After all, clinicians will remind you, the patients are psychotic. How can we expect them to be good tail pinners? Maybe they were listening to voices when they were supposed to be listening to directions, maybe a voice told them to veer to the left instead of walking straight ahead, maybe they have a paranoid delusion about donkeys. In addition to psychotic symptoms causing a tail-pinning deficit, we have medications to consider. If the patients were taking medications (most schizophrenic patients do), these medications may have interfered with their tail-pinning ability. Alternatively, if the patients were hospitalized (most patients are at some point), the process of being institutionalized and removed from society may have had a detrimental effect on tail pinning. Hence the results to clinicians are neither surprising nor terribly informative because the explanations for the deficit seem so obvious.

All these explanations may seem obvious, but they are also wrong. If Pin the Tail on the Donkey is similar to many other neurocognitive tests, we have some surprises in store. If we were to look closer and conduct a series of follow-up studies, we may be surprised to learn that patients perform about the same whether they are experiencing symptoms or not; and that they perform about the same (maybe even a little better) when they are taking medications compared to when they are not. We may be surprised to learn that people with schizophrenia show deficits on this task even before they became schizophrenic, and that family members of the schizophrenic patients, who do not have any psychiatric disorders, show subtle deficits compared with controls.

Simple explanations, even the obvious ones, fall short here. The deficits are not just the result of the symptoms or the treatments of schizophrenia—they are more central to the illness. As we enter the world of neurocognitive deficits, leave your expectations at the door.

Range of the Deficits

Let's consider a sampling of neurocognitive tests that are used in schizophrenia research. The first three areas to be tested (perception, vigilance, and sensory gating) will give us insights into the centrality question. These tests appear to reflect predisposition to the illness and therefore can be used to reveal alternative phenotypes, as described in the previous chapter. The tests are fairly simple; that is, they have a restricted number of task components. The remaining areas to be tested (memory, problem solving, and social cognition) are important because they are associated with a patient's daily activities. Implications of these tests for outcome will be described in chapter 6. All of these are relatively complex tests, and, like Pin the Tail on the Donkey, have many task components.

Perception

Imagine a series of letters flashing across your computer screen. The duration of each letter is extremely brief (in the neighborhood of one hundredth of a second), but you can still identify each letter without much difficulty. Now imagine that after the presentation of each letter, the screen goes completely blank for a brief period, and then some crossed lines appear. Your job is to continue to identify the letters that are presented first and to ignore the lines that follow. If the interval between the two stimuli is short (e.g., less than about one tenth of a second) you may discover that, not only are you unable to identify the letter, you may not even be aware that any letter was presented at all. The letters are called a visual *target*, and the lines act as a visual *mask*. Because the mask came after the target letter, this procedure is called backward masking and it is a measure of visual processing (Breitmeyer, 1984). Figure 4.1 shows an example where the target stimulus (on the left) is presented for 10 milliseconds, followed by a 30 millisecond gap, and then a brief masking stimulus (on the right) that is shown for 20 milliseconds.

Everyone experiences backward masking effects, but individuals with schizophrenia consistently require more time between the target letter and the mask to identify the target accurately (Braff, Saccuzzo, & Geyer, 1991; Green, Nuechterlein, & Mintz, 1994; Knight, Elliot, & Freedman, 1985; Rund, 1993; Schwartz, Winstead, & Adinoff, 1983). Hence they have *deficits* in backward masking. Could this deficit be due to their psychotic symptoms, or to their medications?

It is difficult, if not impossible, to explain masking deficits through psychotic symptoms or treatment (Braff & Saccuzzo, 1982; Green, 1998; Nuechterlein, Dawson, & Green, 1994). First, if we simply compare masking scores with ratings of psychotic symptoms, they do not correlate well (Green & Walker, 1986). Second, people with schizophrenia have pronounced deficits

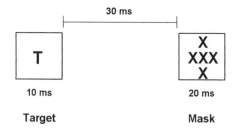

Figure 4.1 ■ *Backward masking. In this task of early visual processing, a briefly presented target stimulus (on the left) is presented for 10 milliseconds, followed by a brief masking stimulus (on the right) that is presented for 20 milliseconds. At very short intervals between target and mask, like the 30 millisecond interval depicted here, the presence of the mask makes it difficult to identify the target. As the interval increases between the target and mask, it becomes easier to see the target.*

even when they are in solid remission and are not experiencing psychotic symptoms (Green, Nuechterlein, Breitmeyer, & Mintz, 1999; Miller, Saccuzzo, & Braff, 1979). Third, unmedicated patients show clear deficits on visual masking—if anything, conventional antipsychotic medication may help performance (Braff & Saccuzzo, 1982; Green et al., 1999). Fourth, siblings of schizophrenic individuals, who do not have any major psychiatric disorders, also show subtle masking deficits (Green, Nuechterlein, & Breitmeyer, 1997). Finally, visual masking deficits are found in people who do not have schizophrenia, but who have mild schizophrenic-like features such as unusual beliefs, magical ideas, or social awkwardness (Braff, 1981; Cadenhead, Perry, & Braff, 1996; Harvey, Keefe, Mitroupolou, & DuPre, 1996). For all of these reasons, visual masking does not appear to reflect the presence of psychotic symptoms or the treatment of the disorder. Instead, performance on this test seems to reflect vulnerability or predisposition to schizophrenia.

Vigilance/Sustained Attention

Laboratory measures of vigilance were developed to address a real-world problem. During World War II, German U-boats were threatening the British coast. British radar operators circled over the North Atlantic trying to identify the U-boats on their radar screens. Their screens were visually "noisy," meaning that many lines and streaks appeared on screen. Some of the lines and streaks were due to imperfections in the equipment; some were real objects—just not the objects that the operator was looking for. Either way, the screen was filled with all sorts of extraneous visual images and the job was difficult.

From the operator's point of view, the U-boats were *targets* and everything else was *noise* (Davies & Parasuraman, 1982). If he concluded that a blip was a U-boat when it wasn't, he could initiate a costly mobilization of defense forces. On the other hand, if the operator concluded that a blip was noise, when it really was a U-boat, the costs to the British population would be even greater. The stakes were very high, any mistake quite serious.

The question for the British Armed Forces therefore couldn't be more practical: How long can an operator perform such a demanding task at an optimum level? A test of vigilance, or sustained attention, was developed. In this test, called the Continuous Performance Test (CPT), the subject looks at a series of stimuli and discriminates which are targets and which are nontargets. The CPT is now a fairly common measure in the study of schizophrenia. Laboratories today with sophisticated computerized CPTs produce visual noise on screens that approximate the perceptual characteristics of World War II radar screens. Figure 4.2 depicts one version of a CPT. Stimuli are briefly presented one at a time over a period of several minutes on a computer screen. A subject responds by pressing a button each time that the target stimulus appears (in this case the number 0) but not pressing for any other stimuli. Vigilance is measured by the ability to distinguish between targets and nontargets.

Not surprisingly, schizophrenic individuals show deficits on the CPT (Nuechterlein, 1991). We cannot explain away this deficit as part of the psychotic symptoms or the treatment of schizophrenia, just as we could not in visual masking. Performance on these types of tests does not change much when people with schizophrenia are in or out of a psychotic episode. In a project from UCLA, Keith Nuechterlein and colleagues administered the

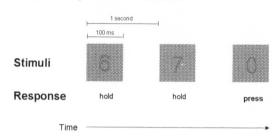

Figure 4.2 ■ *Continuous performance test. In this test of vigilance a series of stimuli are presented briefly, one at a time, and the participant is instructed to press a response button for a particular target. In this case, the target is the number "0."*

CPT to schizophrenic patients during periods of symptom remission and psychotic relapse. Normal controls, who were matched to the patients in terms of age, sex, and race, were tested at the same time as their match. Patients showed a deficit compared to their matched controls at both testing times, and their performance hardly changed as they went from relapse to remission. Other studies have shown that the CPT does not change much when patients are on medications, at least on the conventional antipsychotic medications (Cornblatt, Obuchowski, Schnur, & O'Brien, 1997).

Some of the most convincing evidence about the centrality of CPT deficits for schizophrenia comes from "high-risk" studies (Cornblatt, Lenzenweger, Dworkin, & Erlenmeyer-Kimling, 1992; Mednick, Parnas, & Schulsinger, 1987; Mirsky, Ingraham, & Kugelmass, 1995; Nuechterlein, 1983). In this context, a high-risk study includes individuals who are at higher than normal risk for schizophrenia, but do not have the illness—for example, the offspring of schizophrenic parents. Offspring of patients show deficits on the CPT when compared to a control group. In addition, some of these studies (notably those of Cornblatt, Erlenmeyer-Kimling, and colleagues) followed the high-risk individuals as they grew up and passed through their age of risk for schizophrenia. What they discovered was that deficits on the CPT in childhood predicted later psychiatric problems (Cornblatt et al., 1992; Cornblatt & Erlenmeyer-Kimling, 1985). Apparently, the CPT not only reflects vulnerability to schizophrenia, it may also identify individuals who are most likely to develop problems later.

Sensory Gating

Sensory gating refers to the largely automatic process by which the brain adjusts its response to stimuli. Measurement of sensory gating requires specialized equipment to measure either electrical activity from the brain (i.e., electrophysiology) or muscle activity from the eyelids (i.e., psychophysiology). Let's say you are sitting in a quiet room; suddenly there's a sharp, loud noise. Naturally, you'll be startled. Feeling startled is a subjective reaction, but there is also an objective, measurable component. As sure as death and taxes, you will blink when you are startled. It is possible to measure the size of the blink with a couple of recording electrodes placed around the eyelids. Now, suppose that you hear a quiet, nonstartling tone shortly before the loud noise. This nice quiet tone (called a pre-pulse) has an unusual effect—it reduces the size of the blink (see the top panel of figure 4.3). But this is not true for everyone to the same extent. Schizophrenic individuals show two types of abnormalities on this procedure. First, schizophrenic patients frequently have deficits on these procedures, meaning that the pre-pulse does not reduce their blink as much as it does for normal controls (Braff et al., 1978; Braff et al., 1991; Freedman et al., 1987). Apparently, the first stimulus does not reduce the impact of the second (startling) sound (see the bottom panel of the figure). Second, the amount of sensory gating can be influenced in healthy control subjects by asking subjects to either attend to or ignore the pre-pulse; such instructions, however, have little influence on the sensory gating in schizophrenic persons (Dawson, Hazlett, Filion, Nuechterlein, & Schell, 1993).

In any event, there seems to be some problem in the way patients dampen the impact of a loud stimulus when a quiet tone precedes it. This is known as a deficit in "sensory gating" because

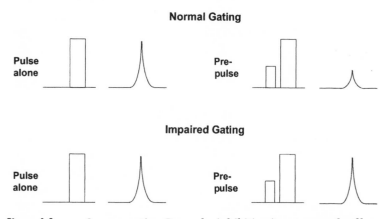

Figure 4.3 ■ *Sensory gating. Pre-pulse inhibition is one example of how to test sensory gating. In this test, a loud noise causes a person to startle, which can be measured with an eye-blink. If a mild tone is presented immediately before the loud tone, the size of the eye-blink is reduced. A deficit in gating is shown in the bottom panel.*

the first stimulus serves as a "gate" for the second stimulus. A sensory gating deficit can be measured by eye-blink, as just described, or by looking at brain electrical activity when two auditory clicks are presented close together. In this case, the brain response to the second click is reduced by the first (similar to the way the pre-pulse reduced the eye-blink). Individuals with schizophrenia fail to show the same degree of reduction as controls do (Freedman et al., 1997).

Deficits in sensory gating may relate to the subjective experiences of the patients who report that they feel "bombarded" by sensory input and cannot filter out the irrelevant stimuli. Abnormalities in sensory gating could help explain the experience: If the impressions of sounds or images are not effectively reduced (or gated), they may be perceived as intrusive and too hard to ignore.

Sensory gating abnormalities are not merely a result of symptoms or medication. They can be seen in unmedicated patients (Hazlett et al., 1998), in first-degree relatives who do not have schizophrenia (Freedman et al., 1987), and in schizophrenic patients when they are in remission (Dawson et al., 1993). For these reasons, one can expect deficits in sensory gating to indicate vulnerability to schizophrenia (Freedman et al., 1999).

Memory

Perhaps no area of neurocognition frustrates and fascinates us as much as memory. Think about the last time you tried to remember where you left your keys or why you went to the grocery store, attempted to learn a new language, or struggled to make a graceful introduction at a high school reunion. In each instance, you were keenly (even painfully) aware of the limitations of your own memory. We are also aware that as we age, our memory is not what it used to be. Mark Twain commented that as a youth he could remember anything, "whether it happened or not." But as he got older and his faculties weakened, he could only remember the things that never happened.

A firmer (but not yet solid) understanding of memory is surely one of the crowning achievements of modern neuroscience. Because of recent advances, we now know that different types of memory exist and that particular neural systems underlie them (Fuster, 1989; Goldman-Rakic, 1993). Memory was once an overlooked deficit in schizophrenia—even the visionary Bleuler mistakenly claimed memory in schizophrenia was intact. Schizophrenic individuals have clear memory deficits and the size of the deficits may be even larger than for other areas of neurocognition (Gold, Randolph, Carpenter, Goldberg, & Weinberger, 1992; Heinrichs & Zakzanis, 1998; Saykin et al., 1991).

Memory demands are omnipresent in everyday situations. Let's say that your spouse wants to prepare dinner and asks you to pick up 15 items from the grocery store. Remembering the list of items involves one type of memory (secondary or explicit memory). After you return home, you realize you've forgotten some of the essential items for dinner, so the two of you decide to eat out. (I know that in real life you would have been humbled and sent back to the store, but indulge me.) Your spouse tells you the phone number of a preferred restaurant. As you walk to the phone, you mentally rehearse the number. But as soon as you make the call, the number is forgotten. Remembering the phone number uses another type of memory (immediate or working memory). There are standardized tests for both these types of memory. Secondary memory can be assessed with lists of words or brief stories (such as short newspaper stories). Immediate or working memory can be assessed by asking someone to repeat a series of digits, or to repeat them in the reverse order they were presented. Schizophrenic patients show deficits on all these types of tasks. The memory deficits may be particularly important for the daily functioning of patients. As we will see in chapter 6, memory (both secondary and immediate) is associated with acquiring skills in rehabilitation programs, solving social and interpersonal problems, and participating in community social and vocational activities. It appears that memory (in this case, memory of words and digits) serves as a neurocognitive prerequisite for adequate functioning in daily life.

We have other types of memory as well—for example, spatial memory (remembering where you parked your car) or prospective memory (remembering to return a phone call at 4:00 this afternoon). Learning and remembering movements uses a completely different form of memory. Every time you practice a tennis serve, a golf swing, a dance-step sequence, or play the piano or touch-type on a keyboard you are using a type of motor or procedural learning. The old adage that one never forgets how to ride a bicycle is partially true. This activity relies on motor/procedural learning, and in general this type of learning is retained well. We do not know as much about how schizophrenia affects these forms of memory. In fact, schizophrenic patients may not have deficits in all of these areas; they sometimes perform normally on tests of motor/procedural learning.

There is at least one form of memory in which the patients perform normally—retention. Retention is the ability to remember something that is already learned. Patients typically require a longer time to learn something such as a list of words or a passage. However, once it is learned, they do not forget any faster than normal controls. This important observation means that schizophrenic patients are very different from people with dementia, who usually have rapid forgetting. It provides some optimism for rehabilitation in schizophrenia. Even if it takes extra effort to convey information in a rehabilitation program, once the material is learned, patients will hold on to that information as well as anyone else.

Problem Solving/Executive Functions

Schizophrenic patients frequently have difficulty with *executive functioning,* which refers to activities such as planning, problem solving, and alternating between two or more tasks. The term "executive" implies that these abilities are the bosses that run a large collection of neurocognitive abilities; in other words, you need these abilities to run your life. Problem solving and executive functions are frequently measured with card sorting tests, the most common being the Wisconsin Card Sorting Test (Heaton, 1981). In a typical test, subjects are given a deck of cards and asked to sort or match the cards but aren't instructed on how to do so. The subjects must figure out how to make the match based on feedback. Figure 4.4 shows a hypothetical card sorting test.

In our made-up test, you would be asked to match the card in the lower right to one of the two cards above. Notice that the cards differ in a few ways. There are two shapes (square and circle), two sizes (small and large), and two types of borders (curved and straight lines). If you want to match to size or to border, then you would match to the card on the left. If you want to match to shape, then you would match to the card on the right. In a typical card sorting test, you would not be told how to match but instead would have to figure it out based on whether you are told your matches are right or wrong. To make matters more complicated, the matching rules can change without warning. You would then be required to figure out the new rule.

Card sorting tests have been used in studies of outcome and cognitive rehabilitation. Although not as consistently related to outcome as memory measures, the card sorting tests appear to be related to vocational outcome, as well as to success in rehabilitation programs. Card sorting tests can be used in combination with neuroimaging techniques to reveal key brain regions and

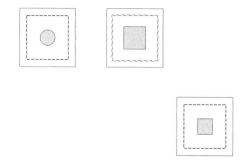

Figure 4.4 ▪ *Card sorting. In a typical card sorting test, individuals are asked to match cards that go together but are not told specifically how to do it. The match is often determined by feedback, which indicates whether a match is right or wrong. In this example, the cards could be matched according to the size of the object, the shape of the object, or the border on the card.*

circuits in schizophrenia. In the next chapter, we will see that card sorting tests are rather good at activating regions in the front of the brain (in the prefrontal cortex) which are thought to be critically involved with schizophrenia (Weinberger, Berman, & Zec, 1986).

Social Cognition—Where Two Worlds Meet

The tests that we have described so far take place in nice, dull laboratories, with nice dull stimuli (e.g., letters, numbers, clicks). This is quite intentional—dullness is a virtue in most experimental testing situations because it keeps the conditions controlled and standardized. In our daily lives, however, perception, attention, and memory usually occur in social and interpersonal situations. Listing words from memory in a laboratory might, or might not, be closely tied to listing past accomplishments from memory during a job interview. Looking for a particular digit in a long series of numbers might, or might not, be closely linked to looking for a friend in a long series of faces coming out of an airport gateway. When neurocognitive abilities take place within social and interpersonal situations, we have a new hybrid area called *social cognition*. Social cognition has several components, including the ability to perceive emotion in others, the ability to infer what others are thinking, and the ability to understand the individual roles and rules that govern social interactions (Penn, Corrigan, Bentall, Racenstein, & Newman, 1997).

When we view interactions through the lens of social cognition, even mundane events become magnificent in their complexity. Consider one of the most common (and delicate) moments of our daily lives—the evening greeting. Every evening around the world, spouses and partners greet each other after long and exhausting days. Before anything meaningful is spoken, a brief, but important, social cognitive event occurs—each person sizes up the mood of the other. All channels of information are fair game for the assessment (posture, voice tone, facial expression), as well as awareness of context (any expectations or prior knowledge about their mood). We do all this in seconds, we usually do it involuntarily, we are usually correct, and our momentary assessment carries a substantial influence on the remainder of the evening's interactions.

Let's start with perception of emotion. Despite some subtle differences, emotion perception is fairly consistent throughout cultures. There are huge cultural differences that influence *if* and *when* someone will show happiness or anger, but there is little difference in how it appears once it is expressed. An angry face looks about the same whether it is encountered while driving in New York City or trespassing in the jungles of the Philippines. Happiness is universally displayed through upturned corners of the mouth, some display of teeth, and narrowing of the eye slit. Figure 4.5 shows two faces that are used in assessments of emotion perception. The one on the right shows a classic surprise while the one on the left shows happiness.

We all learn to recognize the meaning of these emotions, but not everyone learns equally well. People with schizophrenia do not recognize emotion as well as comparison groups do, whether they are looking at a picture (like those in figure 4.5), hearing a voice, or watching a brief videotaped segment. The

Figure 4.5 ▪ *Perception of emotion. These are examples of stimuli used to assess perception of emotion. In 4.5A, the woman is displaying happiness and in 4.5B, the man is displaying surprise. From* The Face of Emotion *(Izard, 1971). Courtesy of Carroll E. Izard.*

reduced ability to recognize emotion takes a social toll. It stands to reason that if someone cannot adequately determine the emotion behind a face or voice, they will not be sure how to respond. Indeed, schizophrenic individuals who have difficulty in recognizing emotion in faces and voices have less social competence (Mueser et al., 1996; Penn, Spaulding, Reed, & Sullivan, 1996). In a collaborative study between the University of Southern California and UCLA, we are finding that emotion perception is also useful in predicting the patients' role in the community, particularly whether or not they can obtain jobs.

For the most part, we do not experience life's interactions like a poker game, with emotion carefully hidden from view. Instead, we are surrounded by a swirl of constantly changing interpersonal cues. We use various neurocognitive abilities to sort through and make inferences about social cues: vigilance to monitor and separate relevant from irrelevant cues, perception to interpret them, and problem-solving abilities to plan a reaction. Emotion perception is just the start of social cognition; it helps us to determine what other people are feeling. But additional processes are needed to determine what other people are thinking, especially what they are thinking about us. Through neurocognitive abilities and knowledge of social and interpersonal situations, we construct ideas about people's dispositions and thoughts. This process is known by the rather abstract name "theory of mind." The breakdown of the theory of mind may be a fundamental deficit in schizophrenia and could help to explain various types of symptoms in schizophrenia, such as paranoia and social withdrawal (Frith, 1992).

A good theory of mind (a knowledge of other peoples' minds) is needed to navigate the waters of our social world successfully. It is also the essence of psychological dramas. The play and classic 1968 movie *A Lion in Winter* depicted the tempestuous relationship between King Henry II (played by Peter O'Toole) and his wife Eleanor of Aquitaine (played by Katharine Hepburn). Henry and Eleanor had a relationship that was not entirely lacking in love, but was entirely lacking in trust, and Henry kept Eleanor locked in prison most of the time. Once a year he let her out of prison for the family Christmas reunion with their three sons. The movie is a story of family intrigue during one of these reunions, as each son schemes to succeed Henry on the throne, while the parents plot with their favorite son. In one scene, Eleanor takes Prince Geoffrey aside to warn him that Henry, who has just renounced his support of Prince John, cannot be trusted. The cynical Prince Geoffrey needs no such a warning, and he responds with a profound socially cognitive statement.

Eleanor: You must know that Henry isn't through with [Prince] John . . . .

Geoffrey: "I know. You know I know. I know you know I know. We know Henry knows; and Henry knows we know it.

We're a *knowledgeable* family."

This clever dialogue from an Academy Award–winning screenplay relies on the unexpected use of the term "knowledgeable." From a social cognitive perspective, however, it is the correct use of the term. Knowledge of what others are thinking appears to be essential for social functioning in our daily lives (even if no kingdoms are at stake).

Searching for Patients with Good Neurocognition

Is schizophrenia always associated with neurocognitive deficits? Not always, and not uniformly. I recall a chronic schizophrenic inpatient who was unable to function in the community, but still routinely defeated the hospital staff at chess. Several patients from our clinical research studies have gone on to competitive jobs and competitive universities. When a large battery of neurocognitive tests was administered to clinically stable patients living in the community, 90 percent showed deficits on at least one neurocognitive domain (such as attention, motor skills, learning, etc.), and about 75 percent showed deficits on at least two domains (Palmer et al., 1997). If we say that deficits on at least two neurocognitive domains indicates impairment, that means that about a quarter of these outpatients did not have prominent deficits. Even if most schizophrenic patients have neurocognitive deficits, a substantial minority of patients do not. This type of finding has raised the question of whether there are subgroups of individuals with schizophrenia who have intact neurocognition.

Not so, according to a team from the NIMH who suggests that neurocognitive deficits are almost always present in schizophrenia but sometimes hard to detect. We discussed MZ (monozygotic or identical) twins in the previous chapter on genetics. If one MZ twin has schizophrenia, the co-twin has about a 50/50 chance of having schizophrenia as well. If the co-twin does not have schizophrenia, the twins are said to be discordant. These MZ twins discordant for schizophrenia constitute a rare and highly informative sample. The group from NIMH gave a neurocognitive battery to the MZ twins. On almost all of these tests, the twin with schizophrenia performed worse than his or her unaffected co-twin (Goldberg et al., 1990). In this study of twins, there was no sign of neurocognitive subgroups. On the contrary, almost all of the twins with schizophrenia performed below where they *should* have been. The non-schizophrenic twin is an ideal control (same genes and rearing family) and provides the best estimate of where the ill twin should have been. Schizophrenia apparently leads to a downward shift in neurocognitive performance.

But if neurocognitive deficits are always present in schizophrenia, how can we understand someone like John Forbes Nash? Nash was born in Bluefield, West Virginia in 1928. In the late 1940s, starting in his early twenties, he revolutionized game theory. He was hailed as one of the most remarkable mathematicians of the second half of the century and is still known today for many of the components of game theory, including the Nash Equilibrium Theory (Nasar, 1998).

At age 30, Nash was about to accept a full professorship at MIT but he suffered a severe psychotic breakdown. He was distant and eccentric to begin with, so some of the signs of his schizophrenia were dismissed as private jokes. His colleagues recall how, in 1959, he walked into a common room at MIT one day and commented that the story on the cover of the *New York Times* contained cryptic messages from inhabitants of another galaxy that only he could decipher. For the next three decades, Nash was in and out of psychiatric hospitals. When he was not in a hospital, he was described as a "sad phantom" who haunted the halls of Princeton "oddly dressed, muttering to himself, writing mysterious messages on blackboards, year after year" (Nasar, 1998, p. 17).

Without warning, Nash started to show signs of recovery in the late 1980s. The reasons for his recovery are still unclear; he was neither taking medications nor seeking help. He started to interact more with mathematicians at Princeton, including several who were old friends. Then in 1994 he received the Nobel Prize in economics, perhaps the only person with a history of schizophrenia ever to do so. He has currently resumed his work as a mathematical theorist.

John Forbes Nash is a true genius and brilliant thinker. His contributions were made prior to the onset of his illness; the disease destroyed his ability for innovative work. So in one sense, Nash is not a neurocognitive exception. However, in another sense, he is. We expect individuals who are predisposed to schizophrenia to show subtle neurocognitive deficits before the start of the illness. Patients, like any other group of people, start out with a wide range of abilities. If someone has an advantageous genetic endowment that places him or her among the top on a particular test or ability, that person can tolerate a reduction in performance due to the illness and still perform in the normal (or above normal) range. Is it possible that Nash showed mild deficits before the onset of symptoms and would have been brighter had he not become ill? If he had a MZ twin without schizophrenia, would that twin have been even more brilliant? For a person who has revolutionized a field and earned a Nobel Prize, such questions do not seem meaningful. It is plausible that at least some individuals with schizophrenia do not experience neurocognitive compromise before the onset of illness. Nonetheless, neurocognitive deficits constitute a key feature of the illness for the majority of patients and, as we will see later, appear to be related to how well patients function in daily life.

Out of One, Many

Although the truth, according to Oscar Wilde, is rarely pure and never simple, explanations are expected to be both. Listing all the varied and disparate types of neurocognitive deficits in schizophrenia leaves one seeking a small number of basic explanations (maybe even one) that can account for the range of performance deficits. When it comes to explanations, the simpler, the better. By analogy, suppose that you are experiencing some health problems. Someone asks you what is wrong. You might say that you are very tired, your muscles ache, you have a sore throat and post-nasal drip, you are having trouble concentrating, you have started watching daytime television, and you are developing a cough. It would be much simpler to say that you have the flu. Not only is that shorter than listing all of the symptoms, it indicates a single cause for the symptoms. One virus has temporarily invaded your body and is wreaking havoc. When it comes to neurocognitive deficits in schizophrenia, we can list all the types of measures on which patients show deficits. Such a comprehensive listing may be impressive, but it does not help us to explain all of the deficits in a parsimonious manner. The goal is to identify a smaller set of core deficits that can explain the diverse range of neurocognitive problems. At this point we have some creative and promising suggestions, including a basic deficit in memory (loss of context), or in attention (reduction in precious resources), or in perception (loss of certain vibrations).

Keeping the Context

Several different groups using very different approaches have concluded that problems in schizophrenia stem from a loss of context. One basic view of context is that it is the overall goal to a series of activities. An early integrative theory of schizophrenia was Shakow's theory of "segmental set," which was developed in the 1930s and 1940s (Shakow, 1946). The idea was fairly simple: Most tasks and daily activities need to be broken into segments. To be successful, one needs to work on the individual segments, while at the same time retaining the mental set for the overall goal. According to Shakow, the basic problem in schizophrenia is that the big picture (the set) tends to be more easily lost or disrupted.

Consider preparing a meal as an example of maintaining set. From a neurocognitive point of view, meal preparation is not a trivial task. Preparing a dinner requires decision making (deciding on the menu), several major steps (shopping, preparing, serving), sequencing of activities (deciding which step takes the longest and what item will be served first), and the ability to switch attention among several tasks that are going on simultaneously. What if suddenly you forget the overall goal? You might start new tasks that have nothing to do with dinner, or not finish those that do. Perhaps you have had a similar experience when, right in the middle of preparing dinner, a friend calls on the phone and you momentarily "forget" the task at hand. Schizophrenic patients sometimes loose track of the overall task, even without an interruption such as a phone call. This is referred to as a loss of set, or in current parlance, loss of *context*.

Research groups, including David Hemsley and colleagues in the United Kingdom (Hemsley, 1987, 1994), have examined memory and context in schizophrenia. The idea here is that our memories form a context for our perceptions. Essentially, a context based on previous experience enables us to organize and assess the significance of sensory input. As new sensory information comes in, it is very rapidly evaluated, based on a context provided by memory (e.g., whether it is important for the current task). If this memory context is weakened, as it may be in schizophrenia, it becomes increasingly difficult to evaluate stimuli. The result is confusion over which stimuli are more important (i.e., relevant) than others.

The most recent incarnation of the context story comes from the area of computer modeling in which programs are designed to simulate the steps that the brain might take to process information. Cohen, Servan-Schreiber, and colleagues developed computer models of neurocognitive tests and simulated what would happen if context was missing. In computer models, this is done by putting in a "context module" and simulating damage to it, much like a deficit in immediate or working memory (Cohen & Servan-Schreiber, 1992; Servan-Schreiber, Cohen, & Steingard, 1996). When computer simulations were compared to the actual performance of schizophrenic individuals, the models were generally quite accurate. People with schizophrenia seem to behave as if their "context module" is not working correctly.

Precious Resources

Attention can be viewed like a reservoir of oil or water—as a limited resource (Kahneman, 1973). People vary in their amounts of this resource (some of us are attention rich, others are attention poor). For the most part, we have a set amount of this resource, although it can fluctuate during the day (and with cups of coffee). We draw on this reservoir when we are performing neurocognitive tasks. But not all tasks are equally demanding. Some, such as performing mental arithmetic, use a considerable amount of this resource; others, such as trimming the hedges, require hardly any.

Nuechterlein and Dawson proposed that many of the deficits in schizophrenia could be explained parsimoniously as the result of a reduced availability of attentional resources (Nuechterlein & Dawson, 1984a, 1984b). Limitations in this attentional resource could arise for several reasons. One is that schizophrenic patients have smaller than normal reservoirs of attentional resources, so there is less to draw on. Another is that they have a normal amount of resources but do not allocate them efficiently. Some of their resources might be tied up in unimportant mental activities and therefore not enough is left over for important activities.

If schizophrenic patients have problems with allocation of attentional resources, we would expect them to show deficits on tasks that require substantial allocation of attentional resources, but to show relatively intact performance on tasks that do not. In general, this is correct for attentional tasks. Patients generally show deficits when attentional tasks are fairly demanding. This might help to explain why remitted patients and their first degree relatives show more consistent deficits on versions of the CPT that require heavy attentional processing, but not on versions that have a minimal processing load. As we will see, however, this attentional resource explanation is not as well suited for explaining deficits on certain tests of early visual perception and sensory gating. These types of tests place fewer attentional demands than tests like the CPT, and they require a basic perceptual explanation.

Picking Up Good Vibrations

The previous explanations of basic deficits in memory and attention are promising. But some of the tasks we discussed earlier, such as visual masking and sensory gating, do not seem to require much attention or memory. Nonetheless, patients still show deficits on these tasks. A parsimonious explanation for these deficits will need to focus on the neural circuits that are responsible for sensation and perception. One intriguing possibility is that these deficits could reflect abnormalities in the way brain activity *oscillates* in schizophrenia. Let me explain.

When we see a visual target in visual masking or hear a sound in the sensory gating measures, a group of neurons fire in response to that stimulus. The neurons, however, fire in a particularly interesting manner: They oscillate or vibrate at a very rapid rate, in the range of 30 to 70 cycles per second (called the gamma frequency range). These oscillations are necessary for perception; they seem to bind features of objects together. Without them, our perceptions of the world would be confusing.

Let's say that you are looking at an object, any object—a painting in an art museum, the desk in your office, or a car in front of you. The visual information from that object is complex (it has different edges, colors, textures), and the visual information in the background is equally complex. You are receiving a plethora of visual information, yet you know exactly what makes up that object, and what does not. It is so easy to perceive a single object as one thing, that we do not realize what an enormous, seemingly impossible, feat it is. The visual information from the painting lands on many different areas of the retina and gets sent to many different parts of the brain. Nonetheless, at no time do you confuse the painting with the wall it is hanging on. Fortunately, at no time do you confuse the car in front of you with the background of other cars. The truly perplexing question is how our brain can take visual information that is related to a single object but is being processed in very different areas of the brain and link this information together so that we perceive one unified object.

The best answer we have at this time is that the different parts of the brain that process visual information from that object are oscillating *in synchrony*. It appears that the synchronization of rapid oscillations at multiple sites in the brain serves to tie objects together and organize our visual world. In the absence of this process, the sensory world would lose its fundamental organization, and we would experience visual and neurocognitive fragmentation.

Several laboratories, including our own, have applied different neuroscience approaches to help determine whether schizophrenia involves a basic problem in either establishing or synchronizing these rapid oscillations. Brett Clementz and colleagues proposed that the sensory gating abnormalities we discussed above might be due to aberrant oscillations (Clementz, Blumenfeld, & Cobb, 1997). Our research team has suggested that the performance deficits of schizophrenic patients on backward masking can be attributed to problems in establishing oscillations (Green et al., 1999). Robert McCarley and colleagues presented audible clicks at varying rates to both schizophrenic individuals and normal controls (Kwon et al., 1999). The researchers then compared the synchronization of brain activity to the different rates of presentation. At the slower rates, brain waves for patients and controls were both synchronized with rate of the stimuli. At the faster rate, the controls continued to show synchronization, but the schizophrenic individuals did not. It was as if their neural firing could not keep up with the increased rate of clicks.

Recall that the quality of connections among neurons plays a critically important role in schizophrenia. The reduction in connectivity would likely lead to a basic problem in the timing and synchrony of neural events (Green & Nuechterlein, 1999a). All of these studies suggest a conclusion not even considered until recently—that a fundamental problem in schizophrenia is the way the brain vibrates.

Summary

In this chapter we have briefly surveyed the key domains of neurocognitive deficits in schizophrenia, including perception, vigilance, memory, executive functions, sensory gating, and social cognition. Some of the measures (e.g., visual masking, the continuous performance test, sensory gating measures) seem closely related to predisposition to the illness and, consequently, may serve as promising alternative phenotypes. Other measures (memory tests and card sorting, and complex tests of social cognition) are related to how well people with schizophrenia manage in their daily lives and will be helpful for understanding outcome in schizophrenia.

In addition, these neurocognitive tests not only provide insights into issues of centrality, genetics, and outcome, they also provide clues about neural underpinnings. The neural processes for many of these tasks are partially understood, at least to the point that some of the key neural pathways involved with the tasks have been identified. In the next chapter, we will discuss how these neurocognitive tests can be combined with rapidly emerging neuroimaging techniques to reveal dysfunctional neural circuits in schizophrenia.

Chapter Five

Neuroimaging and Schizophrenia

Windows on the Brain

Nothing drives home the notion that schizophrenia is a brain disease quite like two noticeably different brain images side by side, one from a person with schizophrenia and one from a non-ill control. Modern neuroimaging techniques are truly dazzling. Some techniques (e.g., magnetic resonance imaging) provide exquisite detail about brain structures, and other techniques (e.g., positron emission tomography and functional magnetic resonance imaging) capture brain function. These neuroimaging procedures can reveal subtle abnormalities in brain structure and function in schizophrenia. For example, they can show what areas of the brain are smaller (or larger) than average in schizophrenia. They can also show differences in the way individuals with schizophrenia activate their brains while performing certain neurocognitive tasks. Neuroimaging has allowed schizophrenia research to move literally from bedside to brain. Enthusiasm for these techniques is understandably high, which is why we should consider what neuroimaging *cannot* tell us about schizophrenia.

First, schizophrenia cannot be diagnosed by a brain scan. Neuroimaging procedures are used for research in schizophrenia, not as part of a standard clinical evaluation. Asking a doctor to determine schizophrenia based on a person's brain scan is like asking a tailor to alter a suit based on a person's neck size. Indeed, there are some differences in brain scans between a group of patients and a group of controls, just as there are expected differences in neck size between people with different suit sizes. But differences in brain structure or function are correlates of the disease, not diagnostic criteria. Few, if any, of the findings mentioned in this chapter are specific to schizophrenia. In fact, some of the findings (e.g., enlargement of the ventricular system or reduced frontal activity) are remarkably nonspecific and are found in a range of disorders. The presence of group differences in neuroimaging may tell us quite a lot about the disease in general, but rather little about any one individual.

Second, neuroimaging can tell us which regions or functions are aberrant in schizophrenia, but they cannot tell us *why*. If a brain region is unusually small in schizophrenia, it could be due to a variety of causes, including early neurodevelopmental processes, head injury, exposure to toxic substances, substance abuse, or an atrophic (deteriorating) process. Furthermore, a brain area might not develop properly if its neural input is reduced from some other region. Hence finding a region that is abnormal in size tells us little about the origins of the problem.

The etiology of functional abnormalities are even more perplexing. Why would a region of the brain not show normal activation on a brain scan during a task? One reason may be that the person is activating other brain regions to accomplish the task. Or perhaps that person is unsuccessfully trying to activate the correct region. The origins of the problem are particularly vague because, as we will see at the end of this chapter, activation during a task always involves a circuit, or interconnected regions. A brain scan can reveal dysfunction in one or more components (nodes) of a circuit, but it cannot indicate the source of a dysfunction. An analogous situation occurs when you are watching television, and the set suddenly turns off. You know the set is dysfunctional, but that's rarely the source of the problem. To isolate the source of the problem you would check progressively larger circuits: the lights in the room, then other parts of the house, then other houses on the street, and finally you could call the electric company. The source of the problem could be anywhere in the circuit (even in a neighboring county or state).

Similarly, neuroimaging may demonstrate that a part of the brain fails to activate properly, but because it is only one component in a large circuit, the root cause of the problem is still unclear.

Early Approaches to Structural Neuroimaging

Despite the newness of many of these techniques, brain imaging has a history that dates back to the early part of the twentieth century. In general, neuroimaging procedures were applied to schizophrenia soon after their development. Hence some of the most robust findings achieved with modern neuroimaging in schizophrenia were established at the time of the Great Depression.

Pneumoencephalography (PEG) provided the first information about brain structure in a living person. In PEG, air is introduced into the subarachnoid space (the space that encompasses the spinal cord and the brain) through a puncture in the lumbar area of the spine. This space is normally filled with fluid called cerebrospinal fluid (CSF) that cushions and protects the brain. PEG involved a careful exchange (CSF coming out and air going in) at the site of the lumbar puncture. Because air is about 800 times less dense than CSF, this procedure increased the visibility on radiography of the spaces normally filled with cerebral spinal fluid. The CSF surrounds our brain for good reason, and its removal with PEG was associated with temporary discomforts such as headaches, nausea, vascular hypotension, and fainting (Oldendorf, 1980).

Despite these drawbacks, PEG provided the first images of the live brains of schizophrenic patients. Figure 5.1, taken from a 1935 article (Moore, Nathan, Elliott, & Laubach, 1935), shows the brain of a 27-year-old woman with a diagnosis of paranoid schizophrenia. She had been continuously ill for 2 ½ years and was described as having experienced "auditory hallucinations, delusions of persecution, and a mild degree of deterioration." The image is noteworthy because of the large, dark areas in both the front and back regions of the brain. The enlargement of these grooves (called sulci, plural for sulcus) can occur when the brain shrinks and leaves too much CSF surrounding the brain.

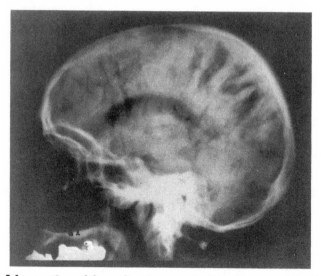

Figure 5.1 ▪ *One of the earliest images of a brain from a schizophrenic patient. We can see that the sulci are unusually large, especially in the frontal and parietal (upper rear) regions. The* American Journal of Psychiatry *92(1), pages 43–67, 1935. Copyright 1935, the American Psychiatric Association. Reprinted by permission.*

In addition to providing early images of the living brain, PEG provided a way to measure the total amount of CSF. Complete removal of CSF from the lumbar puncture was standard for PEG procedures in the 1920s and 1930s, but was stopped for reasons of safety and comfort (CSF is constantly produced, but it takes time to make up for the loss). When the total amount of CSF was measured, schizophrenic patients had more CSF than controls did. So, as early as 1935, PEG revealed that the sulci of the brain were larger than normal and that patients seemed to have too much CSF (Moore et al., 1935). Because CSF fills gaps in the brain, the excess fluid meant that patients had relatively less brain tissue.

Brain Structure in Schizophrenia

Modern neuroimaging techniques have come a long way since PEG. Two commonly used structural neuroimaging techniques are computerized tomographic (CT) scans and magnetic resonance imaging (MRI). The first modern structural scans of schizophrenia involved CT scanning (Johnstone, Crow, Frith, Stevens, & Kreel, 1976), a technique prominent through the late 1980s, when it was largely replaced by MRI. CT scans are like X-rays for the brain, that is, they are adequate for identifying bone and CSF but not very good at distinguishing different types of brain tissue such as *gray matter* from *white matter*. Gray matter consists of the cell bodies of neurons, whereas white matter consists of axons that communicate between neurons. MRI has superior spatial resolution compared with CT and can separate gray matter from white matter. MRI, unlike CT, does not involve any radiation, so it is safe to scan people multiple times.

For the most part, the story of modern structural neuroimaging has been the search for reduced brain size. The early brain scans with PEG suggested that patients with schizophrenia have too much CSF and too little brain tissue. CT and MRI addressed this question by measuring the size of the *ventricles*, which are the spaces within the brain that contain CSF. Because individuals vary in their overall brain size, the most commonly used measure for ventricles is a ratio of the ventricular size divided by brain size (called ventricular brain ratio). Both CT and MRI studies found that individuals with schizophrenia have ventricular brain ratios that are larger than that of comparison subjects, indicating relatively more CSF and less brain tissue (Bilder, 1992; McCarley et al., 1999; Raz & Raz, 1990). Figure 5.2 shows two brains, one from a patient and one from a control. The ventricles are the dark areas in the center of each brain that are filled with CSF. Note that these areas are slightly larger in the patient than in the comparison. Consequently, the amount of brain tissue relative to total brain size is slightly less. Similar to figure 5.1 from 1935, this scan also shows larger sulci in the patient.

The abnormalities in the amount of CSF relative to the brain is a general finding; it doesn't tell us much about which of the many brain regions are reduced in size. For these reasons, scientists have gone well beyond measures of CSF and have closely examined specific brain structures. Some of the most consistent differences in schizophrenia have been found in the temporal lobe,

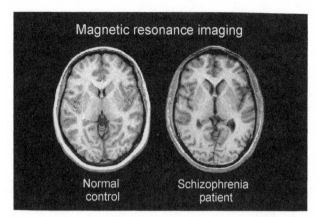

Figure 5.2 ■ *Structural MRI scans from a patient and a comparison subject. The patient shows larger ventricles and sulci. Photo courtesy of Monte S. Buchsbaum, M.D., Mt. Sinai School of Medicine, New York, NY.*

which is the region of the brain closest to the ears (see figure 3 of the color insert). The outer part of this lobe includes the superior temporal gyrus, which is responsible for processing auditory information. This area is often smaller in schizophrenia, and reduced size of this region has been linked to formal thought disorder and hallucinations (Levitan, Ward, & Catts, 1999; Shenton et al., 1992). The inner portions of the temporal lobe include the hippocampus, which is involved with memory. (This structure apparently reminded an early anatomist of a seahorse, which is what the name means in Latin.) Although the hippocampus has an odd shape, it is still possible to measure its size, and some studies find a reduced size in schizophrenia, whereas others do not. When findings across studies are inconsistent like this, it may mean that a difference between groups does not exist, or that one exists, but is so small that many studies miss it. Also, simply looking at the overall size of a structure might not be very informative—we might miss more subtle difference between groups. Similarly, overall body size is one indication of a child's growth, but it is certainly not sensitive to many problems in development. It appears that inconsistent findings with the hippocampus may be because schizophrenia is associated with abnormalities in the shape, not necessarily the size, of this region (Csernansky et al., 1998). A careful examination of a highly detailed MRI revealed that the hippocampus in schizophrenia had unusual shapes, especially around the "head" of the sea horse. The neurons in the head region connect to the prefrontal region, so shape abnormalities probably indicate problems in the connections between the temporal lobe and the prefrontal region.

One way to examine differences between the brains of schizophrenic patients and controls is to compare an average schizophrenic brain (based on combining a large number of scans) with an average control brain. Nancy Andreasen and her colleagues did just this and found that group differences were pronounced in an area of the brain called the thalamus, which is close to the center of the brain (Andreasen et al., 1994). The thalamus is especially critical for communication with the cortex, and for sensory gating; this area is sometimes described as a "relay station" for transmission within the brain. It was suggested that "an abnormality in [the thalamus] could explain most of the psychopathology in schizophrenia, which can be readily understood as the result of abnormalities in filtering stimuli, focusing attention, or sensory gating" (p. 297). Although the thalamus is a critical region for schizophrenia, we will see later in this chapter that it cannot account for all the features of illness by itself, but may be part of a larger circuit.

If schizophrenia involves reduced brain volume in certain regions, there are two general ways the reduction could have occurred. One is that the brain never grew to a sufficient size to begin with (called hypoplasia). Another possibility is that the brain grew to a full size, but then shrank (called atrophy). With schizophrenia, we seem to have both processes operating. Individuals who are experiencing their very first episode of schizophrenia tend to have reduced brain size (Degreef et al., 1992; Lim et al., 1996). In addition, examinations of hospital records show that complications at or around the time of birth (e.g., hypoxia, low birth weight, abnormal fetal heart rate, third-trimester bleeding) are related to subsequent abnormalities in the size (or shape) of brain structure in schizophrenia (Cannon,

Mednick, & Parnas, 1989; McNeil, Cantor-Graae, & Weinberger, 2000). These findings would be expected for a neurodevelopmental illness. The story is more complex for changes after the onset of illness. While some studies find the size of brain structures to be stable over time, others find brain changes after onset of the illness (DeLisi et al., 1997; Gur et al., 1998; Rapoport et al., 1999), which is consistent with a progressive illness. In terms of brain changes, schizophrenia may fit a "progressive developmental" pattern, in which structural brain changes start early in life and continue into adulthood (Woods, 1998).

Positron Emission Tomography (PET)

One of the most remarkable aspects of neuroimaging is the information it can give us about the function, as well as the structure, of the brain in schizophrenia. The roots of functional neuroimaging date back to a discovery made in the early part of the century, to the case of Walter K.

Walter K. was a 26-year-old sailor who went to Peter Bent Brigham Hospital in Boston in 1926 complaining of headaches and failing vision (Fulton, 1928). When physicians placed a stethoscope over the back of his head, they heard a strange sound from the left occipital region. It was a bruit, a sound that occurs when normal blood flow is disrupted. The bruit was caused by a tumor of the left occipital lobe. An operation was attempted, but the tumor could not be removed due to hemorrhaging. The patient recovered from the operation (no small feat in those days) and was seen 16 months later on a follow up visit. The bruit was still audible, but it was not constant. Instead, it depended on what Walter K. was looking at. Dr. Fulton, his perceptive physician, reported this most unusual situation in detail.

> On listening to the bruit, it was obvious that it was much louder than when first examined on the day of entry. Subsequent observations were made during the following week, and it was not difficult to convince ourselves that when the patent suddenly began to use his eyes after a prolonged period of rest in a dark room, there was a

prompt and noticeable increase in the intensity of his bruit. (Fulton, 1928, pp. 314–315)

Even more remarkably, the changes in the bruit seemed to be specific to visual stimuli, and not just sensory stimuli in general.

Activity of his other sense organs, moreover, had no effect upon his bruit. Thus, smelling tobacco or vanilla did not influence it, straining to hear the ticking of a distant watch produced no effect, and ordinary quiet conversation was without demonstrable influence. (Fulton, 1928, p. 315)

These observations stemmed from an unusual situation, a tumor on the part of the brain that processes visual information. Walter K.'s experience indicated that changes in mental activity (in this case, what he was looking at) were accompanied by changes in blood flow to specific regions of the brain. His experience demonstrated that there is a connection between what one is thinking or sensing, and how much blood is flowing into regions of the brain.

The first study of functional neuroimaging in schizophrenia occurred in 1948, when Seymore Kety and his colleagues examined cerebral blood flow. In this study, subjects inhaled a mixture of oxygen, nitrogen, and nitrous oxide. Cerebral blood flow was estimated by the difference in nitrous oxide between the blood going into the brain versus out of the brain. In this early study, the patients did not differ from controls. This study, however, is not really comparable to modern neuroimaging, since it only looked at blood flow for the entire brain, not for specific brain regions. The authors astutely noted that if it were possible to look at blood flow region by region, the findings might be very different. Now, we can look closely at individual regions, and, indeed, the findings are different.

In PET, a person is injected with a radioactively labeled substance that makes its way through the blood stream into the brain. Once in the brain, the labeled substance emits a tiny particle called a positron, which travels only a very short distance before it is annihilated by colliding with an electron (Cherry &

Phelps, 1996). A PET image results from the events that happen at the moment of annihilation—the positron and electron disappear and give rise to two gamma rays that travel in opposite directions, separated by 180 degrees. These gamma rays generally have enough energy to escape the body. Arranged around the individual's head in a large circle are panels with detectors (called coincidence detectors) that register when two gamma rays arrive simultaneously (see figure 5.3). When two detectors are struck at the same time, the source of those photons lies on a straight line called a "line of response" between the two detectors. By combining many different lines of response from different angles, it is possible to obtain an image of brain activity. Areas of the brain that emit more positrons are more active and appear "hotter" on PET images.

PET can be used in two different ways—first, to assess how drugs act in the brain (receptor binding), and second, to study how the brain changes (in terms of metabolism or blood flow) when conducting certain mental activation tasks.

Receptor Binding

All the drugs used to treat schizophrenia act upon certain neurotransmitter receptors. Let us briefly review how neurons work. Neurons have one major function—to communicate with other neurons. They also have other functions common to all cells (such as house cleaning activities and generating energy), but their ability to communicate makes them unique. Neurons communicate when they are "firing" (that is, when they are active). Packets of chemicals called *neurotransmitters* are then released into the narrow space between neurons, which is called the *synapse*. For psychopharmacology, this is where the action is. Neurotransmitters serve as tiny messengers that quickly cross the synapse from one neuron to the other, where they bind briefly to the second neuron. They bind at the *receptor*, thereby causing a change in the second neuron, which can either increase or decrease the likelihood that the second neuron will fire (these effects are called excitation or inhibition, respectively). When a neurotransmitter binds to a receptor, it brings about a physical

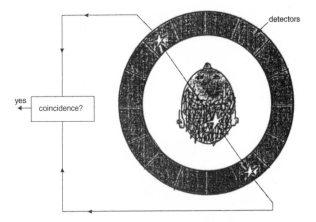

Figure 5.3 ■ *A PET scanner contains an array of coincidence detectors that are placed around the head. The coincidence detectors are connected with fast-timing circuits that look for two simultaneous events on opposite sides of the head. Detection of two simultaneous gamma rays defines a "line of response," which is used to locate the origin of the positron. From Cherry & Phelps, 1996.*

change in the membrane of the second neuron. The neurotransmitter functions like a key fitting into a lock (receptor) that allows a door (membrane channel) to open.

Psychoactive drugs given for the treatment of schizophrenia have a certain tendency to bind to a receptor, which is known as their *affinity* for that receptor. For example, all of the antipsychotic medications have some affinity for the dopamine receptor, and newer medications have an affinity for the serotonin receptor as well. When a drug binds to a receptor, one of two things can happen. The drug may act just like the neurotransmitter and bring about a change in the membrane of the second neuron. In this case, the drug acts like a master key in a lock. When it mimics the actions of a neurotransmitter, it is called an *agonist*. Alternatively, the drug may fit into the receptor, but fail to bring about any change in the membrane. The drug takes up space and prevents the real neurotransmitter from binding to the receptor. In this case, the drug is acting more like a defective key, which fits into a lock but cannot turn. As long as it stays in the lock, nothing else, not even the correct key, can work. This type of drug is called an *antagonist* because it antagonizes, or works against, the system. Antipsychotic drugs are thought to reduce clinical symptoms through their antagonism of the dopamine (and perhaps serotonin) receptor. (There are many subtypes of dopamine and serotonin receptors, which we will consider later.)

PET can explore the binding properties of drugs through the use of radioactively labeled molecules, called ligands. These ligands bind to receptors, just like neurotransmitters, and they release the positrons that are essential for a PET scan. If someone is given a ligand that binds to the dopamine receptor, we can see the location of these dopamine receptors on a PET scan (as in the left panel of figure 4 on the color insert). If an antipsychotic drug with affinity for the dopamine receptor is administered, that drug will bind to a certain percentage of dopamine receptors. If the ligand is injected after the drug is given, the second PET scan will be different (as in the right panel of figure 4). The ligand can only bind to the receptors that are available (that is, unoccupied). In the figure, 74 percent of the receptors were occupied and as a result, the PET scan shows a noticeable decrease in activity.

The dopamine subtypes are identified in a practical, if not inspiring fashion: they are numbered (D1, D2. . .). Using PET studies like those described above, Shitij Kapur and colleagues have shown that all of the antipsychotic medications (including the new ones) have an affinity for the D_2 receptor (Kapur, Zipursky, Jones, Remington, & Houle, 2000; Kapur, Zipursky, Jones, Shammi, et al., 2000). The new medications also show affinity for the serotonin receptor (the 2_A subtype). It appears that the antipsychotic effect of medications start when the dopamine receptors are about 60 percent occupied. That is the good news. The bad news is that side effects such as tremor and muscular rigidity start at about 80 percent occupancy. In other words, there is a rather narrow window of opportunity between 60 percent and 80 percent occupancy in which one can expect therapeutic effects without side effects. With newer antipsychotic medications, which have much lower rates of side effects, it seems much easier to stay in the range of 60 to 80 percent occupancy.

Researchers believe that antagonism of the new medications at the serotonin receptor makes this possible, although we are not entirely sure why.

PET Activation Studies

One of the most fruitful scientific unions of the last decade has been between neurocognition and functional neuroimaging. It is, as they say, a marriage made in heaven. The union has brought to the same table cognitive scientists—with their devotion to measurement of pure neurocognitive constructs—and neuroimaging experts, who have steadily developed techniques to capture ever smaller structures in the brain at ever faster speeds.

Functional neuroimaging usually relies on an activation task—a mental activity that a subject performs during the brain scan. The goal is to capture a picture of the brain while it is conducting that particular mental task. Conducting these studies appropriately is difficult because they require a clear understanding of three things: the task, the imaging procedure, and how the two fit together. These studies frequently fail, not because of the complexities of the imaging technique, but because the activation task is not adequately understood.

Depending on the type of substance injected into the bloodstream, PET neuroimaging can measure either metabolism or blood flow. If labeled glucose is used, it gets picked up by cells that are trying to obtain regular glucose for fuel; the scans, therefore, reveal regions of heightened metabolic activity. If labeled water is used, the scans reveal changes in brain blood flow. Blood flow and metabolism are clearly different but related processes that are associated with mental activity and effort.

Initially, studies with PET in schizophrenia measured metabolism with labeled glucose. The PET glucose scans had reasonable *spatial resolution* (how clear and detailed the image is), but *temporal resolution* (how quickly the image can be obtained) was poor because temporal resolution depends on the half-life of labeled glucose, which is about 110 minutes. These PET studies frequently found reduced metabolic activity in the cortex as well as subcortical areas such as the thalamus (Buchsbaum et al., 1996). Most commonly, reduced activity was found in the frontal brain areas in schizophrenia, a pattern called hypofrontality (Andreasen et al., 1992; Buchsbaum et al., 1992; Gur & Pearlson, 1993). Unfortunately, hypofrontality in schizophrenia is hard to interpret because it is remarkably nonspecific; other conditions such as chronic alcoholism, autism, Alzheimer's disease, as well as exposure to organic solvents are also associated with hypofrontality (Deutsch, 1992). It is as if the frontal region is the first to slow down when a brain is not working right, for any reason.

Later PET studies used labeled water. The half-life of labeled water is much shorter than glucose (only a couple of minutes), so one can obtain images faster and the images can capture briefer mental processes. In one study, labeled water (also called O15 PET) was used to study the problem of selective attention in schizophrenia (O'Leary et al., 1996). Schizophrenic patients and controls were administered a dichotic listening test, in which one word or syllable is presented to the right ear while a different word or syllable is presented simultaneously to the left ear. For example, the word "dog" might be presented to one ear and the word "dock" to the other. This type of test was initially developed to examine the performance of air traffic controllers who frequently encounter multiple streams of conversations simultaneously. People have a tendency to hear the syllables that are presented to their right ear because it projects primarily to the left hemisphere, which processes language for most individuals. This performance advantage for the right ear is much larger if people are making an effort to attend specifically to their right ear.

In the PET study with labeled water, participants were given one condition in which they heard the same word in both ears, and a second condition in which they heard different words and were asked to attend to their right ear. The results (shown in figure 5 of the color insert) show that the brain activation of the patients (in the left two columns) was about the same in these two conditions. Not so for comparison subjects, who showed much more activation in the left regions of the brain (specifically

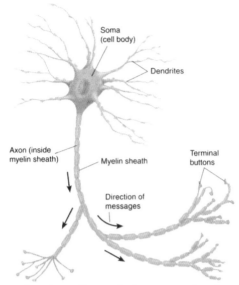

Figure 1 ■ *A drawing of a typical neuron, showing the cell body, dendrites, and axons. From Neil R. Carlson,* Physiology of Behavior, *7th ed. Copyright © 2001 by Allyn & Bacon. Reprinted/adapted by permission*

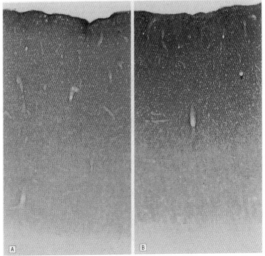

Figure 2 ■ *Stains of synaptophysin, a membrane protein that is critical for transmission at the synapse. The brain of a schizophrenic patient (panel a) contains less synaptophysin than one from a comparison subject (panel b), suggesting that reduced connectivity occurred. From Glantz & Lewis, 1997. Courtesy of the American Medical Association.*

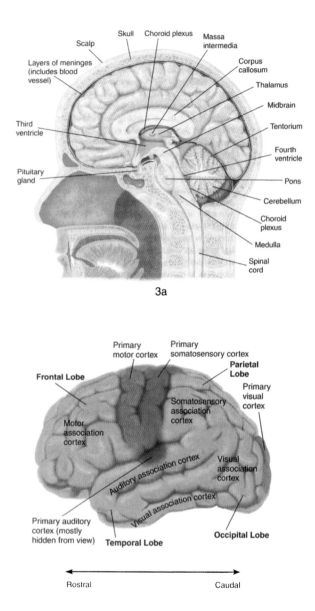

3a

3b

Figure 3 ■ *Two diagrams of key brain structures. Figure 3a is a midline view of the brain and spinal cord. Figure 3b is a lateral view showing the four main lobes and other key regions. From Neil R. Carlson,* Physiology of Behavior, *7th ed. Copyright © 2001 by Allyn & Bacon. Reprinted/adapted by permission*

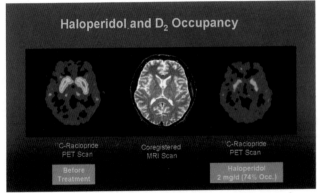

Figure 4 ▪ *PET and drug-binding properties. A PET scan shows where the ligand C-raclopride binds to dopamine receptors before and after an individual received the antipsychotic haloperidol. The scan on the right is lighter because C-raclopride can only bind to unoccupied receptors and haloperidol is occupying 74% of the dopamine receptors. Slide courtesy Dr. Shitij Kapur, CAMH, University of Toronto (Kapur et al.,* American Journal of Psychiatry *2000; 157: 514–20).*

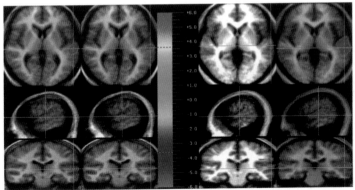

Figure 5 ▪ *PET and selective attention. This figure includes three views of brain activity in patients (two columns on the left) and comparison subjects (two columns on the right). The first column for each group shows activity when the same word is presented to both ears; the second column shows activity when two different words are presented and participants are asked to attend to the right ear. Patients show similar activity in both conditions, whereas the comparison subjects show more activity on the left side when asked to attend to the right ear. Left and right are reversed in this figure according to radiological convention. From O'Leary et al. Auditory attentional deficits in patients with schizophrenia: A PET study.* Archives of General Psychiatry 53, 1996: 633–641. *Courtesy of the American Medical Association and Nancy C. Andreasen, M.D., Ph.D.*

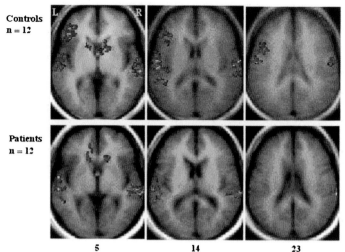

Figure 6 ■ *Activation maps from fMRI during a verbal working memory task for a groups of patients (bottom row) and controls (top row) at three different levels in the brain. The controls show activation in several regions of the left frontal lobe; patients show reduced activity in these areas. From Stevens et al., 1998. Photo courtesy of A. Stevens, Ph.D., and the American Medical Association.*

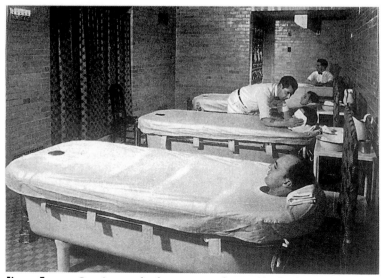

Figure 7 ■ *Continuous baths were one form of hydrotherapy in which patients were placed in a hammock inside a tub. Attendants regulated temperature and water flow.*

the superior temporal gyrus that processes sounds) when they were asked to attend to the right ear. It appears that the brain activation patterns in schizophrenia do not respond to the attentional control of the patient. This is akin to driving a car that continues to go straight, even when you are trying to turn the steering wheel to the left. The study with PET shows how it is now possible to take a neurocognitive deficit in schizophrenia (abnormality in selective attention) and visualize that deficit at the level of specific brain regions.

Functional neuroimaging has been used mainly with mental activation tasks like those just described. However, it is also possible to examine differences in regional blood flow associated with different symptom patterns. In other words, it is also possible to treat the symptoms of schizophrenia as if they are activation tasks. Peter Liddle, Christopher Frith, and their colleagues divided patients according to the three symptom clusters that were described earlier in this book (psychotic, negative, and disorganized) and examined their PET images. They found that negative symptoms were associated with activity in areas of the left prefrontal cortex, disorganized symptoms with areas of the right prefrontal cortex, and psychotic symptoms with the middle portions of the temporal lobe (Liddle et al., 1992).

Other studies have examined specific symptoms that can start and stop, such as hallucinations, while the patient is in the scanner. One study with PET that focused on auditory hallucinations found activity in deep structures under the cortex (e.g., thalamus, sections of the basal ganglia, hippocampus) during hallucinations (Silbersweig et al., 1995). Activation also occurred in cortical regions but varied in location from patient to patient, perhaps reflecting differences in the content of the auditory hallucinations.

These studies of the functional neuroimaging of clinical symptoms are starting to give us a handle on the neural substrates that underlie specific symptom patterns. Up until now, our only evidence of psychotic symptoms has been what the patients are willing to tell us. It is possible that each of the characteristic symptoms of schizophrenia has its own patterns of brain activation. Perhaps some day we will determine the efficacy of medications or appropriate drug dosage through the use of neuroimaging tools. But for now, these tools are strictly for research.

Magnetic Resonance Imaging

Magnetic resonance imaging (MRI) started out strictly as a structural imaging tool. With MRI, an individual is placed inside a large tube-shaped scanner. The scanner creates a very strong magnetic field; it is so strong that people cannot wear any jewelry or metal near the scanner, and the number of credit cards accidentally erased with this technique is legion. The magnetic field has a key function: It causes protons from water molecules in the brain to align. Once a person is in the scanner and the protons are aligned, a brief radio frequency pulse is then applied. The radio pulse pushes protons out of alignment, and for a moment, causes them to spin together in a coherent fashion. This coherence is detected as a signal from a recording coil that is placed around the head. Through a series of complex mathematical operations, the signal can be used to generate images. As the protons lose their coherence, the signal decays. Fortunately for science, different types of tissues (white matter, gray matter, CSF) vary in their rates of signal decay. MRI takes advantage of this difference in decay rates and can yield wonderfully detailed images of the brain.

Functional MRI (fMRI)

The *functional* MRI (fMRI) procedure is a variant of structural MRI. It capitalizes on the fact that blood has slightly different magnetic properties depending on whether it is oxygenated (with oxygen) or deoxygenated (without oxygen). When the brain is active, as when one is performing a mental task, there is an increase in blood flow to a particular region of the brain, although there is not a comparable increase in oxygen consumption. No one is sure why this is so, but it presents a great opportunity for neuroimaging. The increased blood flow without a proportional increase in oxygen consumption means that venous blood (blood in the veins leaving a particular brain region) has higher oxygen levels during times of mental activity. In times of low mental activity, the venous blood has lower levels of oxygen (see figure 5.4). This difference in oxygenated versus deoxygenated venous blood yields a small increase in MR signal (roughly 2 to 5 percent at a moderate magnetic field of 1.5 Tesla). So, fMRI uses these small differences in blood oxygen levels to obtain images that are based on the difference between activated and nonactivated mental states.

There are high expectations for the applications of fMRI to schizophrenia research. The fMRI procedure is faster (better temporal resolution) and clearer (better spatial resolution) than PET. The temporal resolution is so good (down to a tenth of a second for a single slice) that it is now possible to obtain whole-brain imaging of moderately brief neurocognitive processes (Cohen & Bookheimer, 1994), although for very brief neurocognitive processes (such as early visual and auditory processing) fMRI is still a little slow, and electrophysiological methods are preferred. Because fMRI does not involve radiation, scans can be repeated safely within a session or across sessions. Also, fMRI is well suited for examining brain activation in a single subject (PET activation typically relies on groups of subjects).

The application of fMRI to schizophrenia is still relatively recent, but intriguing findings are starting to emerge. A group of scientists from Yale used fMRI to study a type of memory, auditory working memory, in individuals with schizophrenia and comparison subjects. We will see in the last chapter that deficits in auditory working memory are linked to how well patients function in their daily lives. In the study, participants were presented with a list of four words while in the MRI scanner. Following a brief delay interval, one of the words was repeated. Participants were told to indicate the order that the repeated word had originally appeared (i.e. first, second, third, fourth) by holding up the corresponding number of fingers. Figure 6 of the color insert shows the results of the fMRI for controls (top row) and patients (bottom row) at three different levels of the brain (Stevens, Goldman-Rakic, Gore, Fulbright, & Wexler, 1998). The task clearly activated regions of the frontal lobe for the comparison subjects, but not for the patients. It is clear that fMRI, like

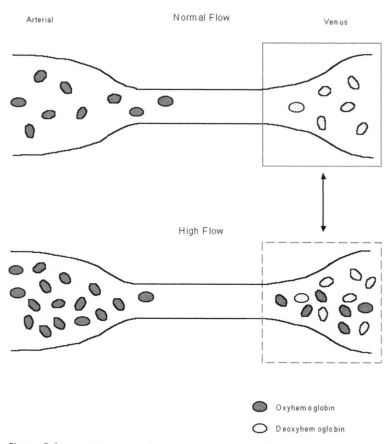

Figure 5.4 ■ *Diagram of the oxygenated and deoxygenated blood in veins during a period of mental rest (top) and activity (bottom). Notice that during rest, the venous blood has low levels of oxygenated hemoglobin; in periods of mental activity, these levels are higher and have different magnetic properties.*

PET, can be used to identify the neural regions that underlie a particular neurocognitive deficit in schizophrenia, in this case, auditory working memory. These neuroimaging studies can identify neural substrates for neurocognitive deficits that are common in schizophrenia, but they do not necessarily identify the neural substrates of schizophrenia per se. Because many other disorders show comparable neurocognitive deficits, these procedures are highly informative, but not diagnostic.

Magnetic Resonance Spectroscopy (MRS)

Neuroimaging techniques not only tell us what parts of the brain are active with a certain task, one form of magnetic resonance also tells us about the chemical composition of brain areas (Salibi & Brown, 1998; Thomas & Alger, 1997). Like MRI, magnetic resonance spectroscopy (MRS) involves placing a person in a scanner that has a strong magnetic field and causes an alignment of particles. In standard MRI, the signal comes from the nucleus of hydrogen in water molecules (i.e., protons), but in MRS the signal comes from the nuclei of molecules and chemical structures other than water (i.e., phosphate groups). MRS is based on the fact that the MR signal molecules generate is affected by the electrons that surround them. You may recall from high school chemistry that an atom has a nucleus, which is surrounded by a certain number of fast-moving electrons. These electrons have a negative charge and are so tiny and move so fast, that they are often considered to be a "cloud" that envelops the nucleus. For MRS, the important point is that this electron cloud sets up its own tiny magnetic field that can shield the nucleus. Just as a real cloud blocks sun light, the electron cloud blocks very slightly the magnetic field in the scanner. The amount of shielding differs from molecule to molecule, depending on several factors such as how many electrons are in the cloud. Hence each molecule has its own magnetic resonance signature and can be measured by the amount of shielding present (called the chemical shift because it causes a detectable shift in the MR signal for that region). By measuring the amount of shift, certain chemicals can be identified and located in the brain.

MRS is a relatively new technique and few studies have applied it to schizophrenia, but the results are consistent with other types of neuroimaging studies. One chemical that has been examined in MRS studies is NAA (for N-acetyl-aspartate). Although the exact role of this substance is not understood, it seems to be a marker of neuronal health. Compared to control subjects, individuals with schizophrenia have reduced levels of NAA in the hippocampus and the prefrontal region, but not other regions (Bertolino et al., 1996). Such a finding suggests neural pathology in these areas. The hippocampus and prefrontal region have strong connections with each other, and are frequently reduced in size or dysfunctional in schizophrenia. Later in this chapter, we will consider whether these two regions may comprise a neural circuit that is problematic in schizophrenia.

Diffusion Tensor Imaging

To grasp the idea behind diffusion imaging, imagine watching a film of two people playing a game of racquetball. You watch as they move around the court, and after the game is over, you see them walking back to the locker room through a narrow corridor. Now imagine that you watch the film again, this time fast-forwarding it so that you can see the players, but not the ball. What would it look like? During the game you would see the two players running all around the court in what appears to be a random fashion. They would appear to move in all directions without any particular pattern; they would not systematically run to the left or swirl in a clockwise fashion. However, once they were in the corridor, their motion would become much more constrained and predictable. They might sway a little to the left or right, but mainly walk straight ahead along the corridor.

Water molecules in cells act essentially the same way. When water molecules have large spaces (like a racquetball court), they move in all directions in an unconstrained fashion. This is called a high level of diffusion. Once the molecules are in a narrow passage, they have few choices and mainly move along the length of the passage. In this case, their diffusion is low. Recently, a new type of MRI called diffusion tensor imaging was developed that can measure the amount of diffusion of water molecules in different parts of the brain. The parts of the neuron that are involved with communication, such as axons, create narrow passages. The greater the amount of narrow passages (axons), the more communication is going on among neurons, and the less the amount of diffusion of water molecules.

Kelvin Lim and his colleagues have applied diffusion tensor imaging to a group of schizophrenic patients and a comparison group (Lim et al., 1999). The patients' brains showed more diffusion in all of the regions studied, including the frontal, temporal, parietal and occipital regions. This pattern suggests fewer axons that comprise the white matter in the brain and consequently less communication among neurons in schizophrenia. The patients, however, did not have an overall reduction in white matter, that is, the volume of white matter was about the same as that of controls. Diffusion tensor imaging revealed a problem in neural communication that was not detectable simply by looking at the volume of connective fibers—it provided a special measurement of diffusion that tells us how well these neurons were doing their job of communicating with other neurons. We considered a wealth of indirect evidence for reduced neuron communication in chapter 2. This new type of imaging provides more direct measurement of neuronal communication in the living brain.

Disrupted Brain Regions versus Neural Circuits

The studies of neuroimaging in schizophrenia typically suggest that a certain brain region is dysfunctional or aberrant in the illness. We know, however, that schizophrenia is not like a typical neurological condition, such as a stroke or tumor, in which brain tissue is effectively destroyed. There are no holes in the brain of a person with schizophrenia. Instead of focusing on one region or another, it will be more informative to locate one or two networks in schizophrenia that do not communicate adequately. Over the past decade, a fundamental shift has occurred in the neuroimaging of schizophrenia, as scientists search for disconnected circuits instead of dysfunctional regions. It is no secret that brain regions act in concert, not isolation. So why is the focus on circuits a relatively new development? Because studying circuits is hard.

The search for dysfunctional circuits in schizophrenia has proceeded in a few different ways. One way is to use animal models of schizophrenia. Let us look at the pre-pulse inhibition of the startle blink (PPI), which we discussed in the last chapter. This deficit has been linked to schizophrenia, and is a promising alternate phenotype for genetic studies. Importantly, the PPI procedure can be used across an entire mammalian spectrum: from mice to rats to college sophomores. Applying PPI to rats and mice can yield detailed information on the neuroanatomy of the underlying circuits. By using this procedure, researchers from the University of California at San Diego have mapped out a circuit that supports PPI, including the cortex, regions below the cortex (regions of the basal ganglia), and thalamus (Swerdlow, Braff, Taaid, & Geyer, 1994; Swerdlow & Koob, 1987). Once again, such a network is not considered a circuit for schizophrenia per se; rather it is a circuit for a schizophrenia-linked neurocognitive deficit.

An advantage in using animal models to study schizophrenia-linked deficits is that investigators can then influence one of the regions in the circuit with site-specific neurochemical infusions. Regions involved with the circuit can be discretely lesioned, and the effects can be selectively reversed with drugs, including candidate antipsychotic drugs. For example, the ability of antipsychotic medications to reverse deficits in PPI correlates with their clinical potency. Thus, the animal models are not only highly useful for isolating certain components of a schizophrenia-relevant circuit, they are also useful for selecting new medications.

In addition to animal models, key circuits can be identified with the neuroimaging procedures discussed in this chapter. Sometimes a pattern of deficits shows up across the same brain regions with such regularity that the regions appear to act like a connected circuit. The regions are considered "nodes" and it is often easier to identify dysfunctional nodes than circuits. A node would be comparable to a hub for an airline: It is one of the key connecting points for the circuit. Along these lines, Nancy Andreasen and colleagues have proposed that the key circuit for schizophrenia involves the prefrontal cortex, thalamus, and the cerebellum (a cauliflower-shaped organ at the back of the brain). They suggest that the fundamental deficit in schizophrenia involves a disruption in the fluid coordination of mental activity, a condition they refer to as "cognitive dysmetria" (Andreasen et al., 1999; Andreasen, Paradiso, & O'Leary, 1998). Just as certain neurological conditions can disrupt the fluid coordination of movement, so can schizophrenia lead to the mental equivalent— a disruption of mental timing and fluidity. Evidence that this circuit is disrupted comes from a series of neuroimaging studies, especially from PET, which reveal deficits in the nodes of this circuit (prefontal cortex, thalamus, and cerebellum). Based on the evidence for dysfunctional nodes, it is reasonable to conclude that these nodes comprise a dysfunctional circuit, but that conclusion still requires some inference because it is difficult to test the connections directly.

Trying to link an abnormality in one region with a structural or chemical finding in another region is an alternative way to search for circuits. Scientists from NIMH hypothesized that schizophrenia involves a dysfunctional circuit between a lateral part of the prefrontal cortex (the dorsolateral prefrontal cortex) and the temporal lobe. They started with an important finding: When patients perform a card sorting test (the WCST), they do not activate the lateral portion of the prefrontal region as much as controls do (Berman, Zec, & Weinberger, 1986; Weinberger et al., 1986). Such differences between patients and controls were observed in this region on the card sorting test, but not on some other activation tasks.

Because the dorsolateral prefrontal region is linked to the hippocampus, the researchers turned their attention there and measured its volume with structural MRI. They found that reduced volume of the anterior hippocampus was related to the reduced activity in the prefrontal cortex (Weinberger, Berman, Suddath, & Torrey, 1992). In a subsequent study, this group related the level of activation of a prefrontal-temporal network elicited with card sorting to MRS findings from the dorsolateral prefrontal cortex. As mentioned above, MRS has the ability to detect levels of substances in the brain such as NAA that are associated with the overall health of neurons. NAA levels in the prefrontal cortex were correlated with the WCST-induced activation in the prefrontal cortex, parietal lobe, and temporal lobe, suggesting that integrity of neurons in prefrontal cortex is a critical part of a circuit for the card sorting task (Bertolino et al., 2000). Normal comparison subjects did not show this correlation, perhaps because they do not have disease-related pathology in the prefrontal region.

These studies suggest which circuits, as opposed to regions, may be dysfunctional in schizophrenia. Similar to the search for parsimony of neurocognitive deficits described in the previous chapter, the search for dysfunctional circuits in schizophrenia may help to explain a wide array of somewhat disparate findings. Also, the search for circuits fits with what is known to be critically lacking in schizophrenia—connectivity among neurons.

Chapter Six

Interventions for Schizophrenia

Raising the Bar

In Oscar Wilde's play *Lady Windermere's Fan*, a character laments that "In this world there are two tragedies. One is not getting what one wants, and the other is getting it. The last is much the worst." The treatment of schizophrenia has weathered both of these "tragedies," and while the second one may not be worse, it is more perplexing. There is a long history of varied, seemingly desperate, attempts to find treatments for schizophrenia that would place the symptoms under control or make them go away entirely. Starting with the introduction of antipsychotic medications in the 1950s, the goal of symptom reduction was mostly realized for patients. With the exception of a minority of "treatment-resistant" patients who are willing to take the medications but do not respond adequately to them, the first generation of medications reduced and often eliminated the psychotic symptoms of illness. Recently, a new generation of medications has started to chip away at treatment-resistant schizophrenia, and patients with a previously intractable form of schizophrenia are beginning to respond. But a profound lesson learned from hard-fought successes is that symptom reduction by itself is not enough. Reducing or even eliminating the symptoms is important, but it is only a first step.

From a symptom management perspective, successful treatment means that a patient enters a hospital hearing voices, but leaves the hospital without hearing them. Symptom reduction and clinical stabilization is the first order of business for admission units and emergency rooms. Patients tend to be highly agitated when they come to the hospital, and frequently they are brought to the hospital by distraught family members or by police after a public display of bizarre behavior. Although for many years symptom reduction was synonymous with effective treatment, this is generally not true anymore: The bar is being raised. Clinicians, families, and patients themselves want more than just a reduction or elimination of symptoms—they want to see fuller and more productive lives.

The treatment of schizophrenia can be seen as a series increasingly higher hurdles. The first goal is to reduce psychotic symptoms; the second is to reduce negative symptoms; the third is to improve the neurocognitive deficits; and the fourth goal is to reduce disability and improve functional outcome. On average, the first treatment hurdle (psychotic symptoms) is the easiest to achieve, and the last one (reducing disability) is the hardest. These hurdles are not always surmounted in sequence. For example, some patients show improvement in their functional outcome even with persisting symptoms and continuing neurocognitive deficits. At this time, separate treatments for overcoming each of the hurdles do not exist.

Historical Approaches

The first treatments to show undisputed effectiveness for schizophrenia were introduced in the second half of the twentieth century. Prior to this time, the treatments were a series of odd and awkward attempts to manage a baffling illness (see Braslow, 1997 for description). During the early part of the century, mental illness was increasingly seen as a bodily illness, specifically a brain illness, and the treatments reflected this belief. To illustrate this idea, let us consider one form of early therapy for schizophrenia: hydrotherapy.

From the 1910s to the 1940s, the predominant form of therapy for severe mental illness, including schizophrenia, was hydrotherapy. There were two types of hydrotherapy: wet packs and continuous baths. Wet packs involved wrapping patients in sheets that were dipped in water ranging from 40 to 100° F. Agitated patients were wrapped in colder sheets, frail patients in warmer sheets. Patients often went through both cooling and heating phases while in the pack, a process that could take several hours. Continuous baths involved placing patients in a hammock inside the tub (see figure 7 on the color insert). A canvas sheet with a hole cut out for the patient's head covered the tub. Valves allowed attendants to regulate temperature and water flow. Similar to the wet packs, the treatment could last for hours. The doctors who used hydrotherapy saw it as authentic therapy, not merely a matter of restraint, like a straight jacket. Indeed, complex physiological explanations for its effects abounded. Despite the doctors' conviction that this was therapeutic, the patients' views were often quite different. Here, from 1919, is a patient's description of hydrotherapy:

> Two fellows came in, hop-heads, dope-heads, and they gave one of them what you call a continuous bath, . . . I had a room right next to it for a couple of nights and during the day they brought him in and gave him this continuous bath. . . . I don't know his name, they put him in these and had a canvass over this bath-tub where just their head sticks out and then they turn the water on. . . . Smith was giving this man this bath and . . . was making the water so hot that the fellow would holler and the other man would choke him until his tongue held out of his mouth. . . . The next day they took the man to the morgue, poor fellow. (Braslow, 1997, p. 49)

Regardless of the report's accuracy, this patient clearly feared the new treatment. A report from a doctor at the same hospital provides a very different perspective.

> Take a man that is delirious and put him in the tub and keep him there, and by virtue of his condition he thinks

you have got him in scalding hot water, when, as a matter of fact, the temperature is only 92 degrees. The man screams and hollers and swears that you are burning him up alive, and they call you all kinds of names. . . . You simply have to ignore his pleas, that are sometimes heart-rending, and you do your duty by him, and do it in spite of himself. (Braslow, 1997, p. 39)

While the patients may have viewed hydrotherapy as no better than restraints, the doctors were convinced that they were offering something of value. It was, they believed, a treatment that acted directly on the brain. An academic psychiatrist from that period explains in lofty, confident, and scientific-sounding terms that hydrotherapy "is the only scientific treatment for the acute excitement of the insane that has yet been discovered. . . . [Wet packs] act by increasing the elimination by the skin, helping to rid the system of toxins and poisonous matter in the constitution." The doctor went on to explain that hydrotherapy brings "blood to the surface and relieve[s] the congestion in the brain and spinal cord, which in most cases seems to cause the excitement" (Braslow, 1997, p. 47).

Hydrotherapy gave way to other, more direct attempts to alter brain functioning, including malaria induction, insulin-induced coma, and electroconvulsive treatment. The logical extension of this focus on brain processes culminated in a direct assault on the brain—the severing of neural fibers. Prefrontal lobotomy was based on the assumption that psychiatric problems in general, and schizophrenia in particular, arose from fixed abnormalities in the neural tracts leading to the frontal lobes. The idea was that severing the white matter disrupted these fixed maladaptive connections and allowed more adaptive ones to form. In the prefrontal lobotomy, a type of knife called a leukotome severed the connections to the frontal lobes through holes that were drilled in the top of the head, the side of the head, or above the orbit of the eye. Even during its heyday (late 1940s and early 1950s), prefrontal lobotomy was considered extreme and was reserved for patients whose behavior and functioning were unresponsive to the standard treatment. Emily is described as such an example.

> She was born in Texas in 1914, the youngest of five children. According to her older brother, she never got along with her siblings, and he uncharitably described her as a "rattle brain, bull headed, overbearing, and lazy." Her father, a common laborer schooled in "only the bible," moved the family to California in 1929. Fifteen at the time, Emily adjusted poorly to her new home. She dropped out of school and married an older man who would spend most of their marriage in San Quentin State Penitentiary. (Braslow, 1997, p. 125)

Emily had two children and was admitted to Stockton State Hospital in late 1940. She was described by the admitting doctor as "totally irresponsible about the care of her children—has been immoral. During the past few days has been totally irrational most of the time—unable to carry on a rational conversation, or understand one" (Braslow, 1997, p. 125). For over six years, Emily showed uncontrollable behavior, recalcitrance, and assaultive behavior. There was little improvement in her condition despite numerous attempts at therapeutic intervention, including over 450 electroconvulsive treatments. Based on the therapies of the time, she was considered a treatment-resistant patient, and surgery was deemed justifiable. In 1947, she became the first patient to be lobotomized in a California state hospital. Initially, the lobotomy seemed to result in clear improvement. Doctors commented that her assaultive behavior stopped completely and she was friendlier. In a statement that reveals the perspective of the times, she was also described as "more interested in housekeeping." The improvements, however, did not last long, and she was soon back to her previous state. She remained in the hospital another 17 years.

The interventions used in the first half of the twentieth century reinforce the all-too-common stereotype of a malicious psychiatrist inflicting suffering on helpless (and incarcerated) patients. It is important to keep historical context in mind. The diversity of treatments reflect desperate attempts on the part of psychiatrists to find something, anything, to help. Why did well-intentioned doctors continue to use invasive procedures that, in retrospect, were ineffective? Recall that the clinical symptoms of schizophrenia wax and wane, so that spontaneous symptom improvement may coincidently occur at the start of an intervention. If so, a hopeful clinician could attribute improvement to the treatment.

Also, just because a treatment sounds cruel, does not necessarily mean that it is. With electroconvulsive therapy a patient is first anesthetized, and then electrical current is applied to the head to induce a convulsion. This procedure sounds brutal and has been reviled for decades by critics of psychiatric treatments. Many hospitals have abandoned the procedure based on public reactions. But why is it still being used? Because it is a highly effective and rapid treatment for depression. Unfortunately, it is not effective for schizophrenia, the disorder for which it was initially developed.

The treatments of schizophrenia have moved closer and closer to a direct altering of brain functioning (e.g., from hydrotherapy to electroconvulsive therapy to lobotomy). The first truly effective treatment for schizophrenia was a medication that acted directly on the neurotransmitters in the brain. Like many of the treatments for major mental illness, it was discovered by accident.

Drug Interventions for Clinical Symptoms

First Generation Antipsychotic Medications

During the 1940s, Henri Laborit, a French surgeon, was testing new drugs that he hoped might reduce the risk of shock for patients during or immediately following surgery. In 1950, a French pharmaceutical company synthesized a new drug, called chlorpromazine, and sent it to Laborit to try with surgical patients. Chlorpromazine had unusual properties; it was calming, but did not confuse or strongly sedate petients. This was a good thing from a surgical point of view—an injection of chlorpromazine before surgery meant that less general anesthesia was needed and therefore the risk of shock was reduced. Laborit and colleagues said that the drug appeared to create a "disinterest" for the immediate environment. "In doses of 50–100 mg intravenously, it provokes not any loss in consciousness, not any change in the patient's mentality but a slight tendency to sleep and above all 'disinterest' for all that goes on around him. . . . These facts let us foresee certain indications for this drug in psychiatry" (translated in Caldwell, 1970, p. 135).

In their very first publication on the new drug, Laborit and his colleagues suggested a role for chlorpromazine in treatment of psychiatric disorders. Soon thereafter, the first trials of chlorpromazine with psychotic patients were underway, and they confirmed that the drug was effective in treating psychosis. Chlorpromazine became the leading medication in the "first generation" of antipsychotic medications (others include haloperidol, thioridazine, and fluphenazine). These drugs dominated the treatment of schizophrenia for the next 40 years.

These first-generation drugs were very good at one type of intervention—reducing psychotic symptoms, particularly hallucinations and delusions. A subgroup of patients (usually about 20 to 25 percent) did not show an adequate response and were considered treatment-resistant, but most patients responded reasonably well in terms of positive symptom reduction. Although these medications were sometimes called "anti-schizophrenia" medications, they were really antipsychotic medications that did little for other aspects of the illness. For example, they were not very effective at reducing negative symptoms or for reducing the neurocognitive deficits of schizophrenia. Despite their reliable effects on positive symptoms, we will see in the next chapter that these drugs have done little to improve overall functional outcome for patients.

Newer Medications

Starting in 1990, a new generation of antipsychotic medications were introduced in the United States. These newer antipsychotic medications were also good at reducing psychotic symptoms (without efficacy for these symptoms, they would not have been approved for market). Some treatment-resistant patients who were not responsive to first-generation medications showed improvement on the newer ones. Table 6.1 lists these new medications both by brand and generic names (see Weiden, Scheifler, Diamond, & Ross, 1999, for a very readable summary of these medications). We will refer to all of them by their generic name.

Scientists are now learning about the differences between the first-generation medications and the newer ones. The newer drugs appear more effective for negative symptoms and for symptoms such as anxiety and depression that often accompany schizophrenia (Marder, Davis, & Chouinard, 1997). As we will see below, they also appear more effective for neurocognitive deficits. But the most noticeable difference, and the reason the drugs were developed and introduced, is that they have fewer side effects.

Side Effects

The first-generation medications have several types of troubling side effects, most notably, those of involuntary movements (Kane, 1996; Weiden et al., 1999). These medications sometimes cause muscular rigidity and tremor, similar to the signs of

Table 6.1 ■ *Newer antipsychotic medications (in order of introduction in the United States)*

Generic Name	Brand Name	Manufacturer	Year of Introduction in U.S.
clozapine	Clozaril	Novartis	1990
risperidone	Risperdal	Janssen	1994
olanzapine	Zyprexa	Eli Lilly	1996
quetiapine	Seroquel	Astra Zeneca	1998
ziprasidone	Geodon	Pfizer	2001

Parkinson's Disease. The movement side effects are caused by the drugs' ability to block the dopamine D_2 receptor, which is linked to the execution of smooth movements. Akathisia, another side effect, is a form of restlessness that is subjectively uncomfortable for patients. The most serious type of movement side effect is tardive dyskinesia, which is less common than tremor and rigidity but much harder to control. It tends to occur after long-term antipsychotic administration (usually years) and is characterized by slow writhing involuntary movements, especially of the lips and tongue. The common types of movement side effects are listed in Table 6.2 (from Weiden et al., 1999).

Some side effects can be managed by other types of medications. For tremor and rigidity, treatment involves a medication that blocks the acetylcholine receptor (i.e., *anticholinergic* drugs). These types of drugs seem to bring the dopamine and acetylcholine neurotransmitters into a kind of helpful balance. The anticholinergic medications, however, have their own side effects, including dry mouth, blurry vision, and some types of neurocognitive impairment. There is no specific treatment for tardive dyskinesia; however, it can be temporarily suppressed by increasing the dosage of the very medications that cause it.

Before we blame the antipsychotic medications for all of the movement side effects, it should be noted that involuntary movements were observed before the introduction of antipsychotic medications. For example, Kraepelin's definition of "spasmodic phenomena" in schizophrenia sounds just like tardive dyskinesia,

Table 6.2 ▪ *Movement side effects of first-generation medications*

Akathisia	restlessness, inability to sit still
Akinesia	motor slowing
Tremor	shaking, mainly in the hands
Rigidity	muscular stiffness
Dystonia	muscular cramping
Tardive Dyskinesia	uncontrolled movements, mainly of the mouth and tongue

but his description was written fifty years before the advent of antipsychotic medications.

> The **spasmodic phenomena** in the musculature of the face and of speech, which often appear, are extremely peculiar disorders. Some of them resemble movements of expression, wrinkling of the forehead, distortion of the corners of the mouth, irregular movements of the tongue and lips, twisting of the eyes, opening them wide, and shutting them tight, in short, those movements which we bring together under the name of making faces or *grimacing*; they remind one of the corresponding disorders of choreic patients. (Kraepelin, 1971, p. 83)

Likewise, the same types of tremor and rigidity associated with drug administration have been observed in patients who are experiencing their first psychotic break and who have never been medicated (Chatterjee et al., 1995). Hence schizophrenia itself might be associated with movement disorders. If so, the older antipsychotic medications are probably exacerbating, not causing, certain types of movement disorders for patients.

The outlook for the newer medications is more promising because their side effects are generally much milder. Although clozapine has essentially no movement side effects, its introduction in the United States was delayed for many years because of a potentially fatal side effect called agranulocytosis, which involves white blood cells. Regular monitoring safeguards against this condition, but some patients object to the frequent blood draws that accompany the prescription of this medication. Some of the newer drugs have movement side effects similar to conventional medications, but the side effects are milder and occur at relatively high doses. Another problem with the newer medications is the possibility of weight gain, which is not only undesirable from most patients' point of view, but can also increase health risks in some patients (e.g., those prone to diabetes).

Side effects are not only sources of discomfort, they are also one reason why patients sometimes stop taking medication. After all, no one wants to take a medication that makes his or her hands shake, causes restlessness, or promotes weight gain. On the other hand, the risk of relapse is much higher when patients (especially chronic patients) are not taking medication. The problem with adherence to medication is a constant worry for both clinicians and families. Here a concerned mother poignantly describes the consequences:

> I feel strongly that people with schizophrenia should stay on their medication. If legal ways were implemented to force people to stay on medication, fewer would get into trouble in the community. Moreover, the cost of restabiliz-ing patients who repeatedly go off their medication is an expense that is becoming harder to justify.... One time our daughter [went off medications and] decided to try faith healing. Some days we hardly saw her. Her brother noticed one day that we had not seen her for 3 days. He went to investigate and found her in bed, very thirsty and very hungry. She told him the "aliens" had placed force fields around her ankles and wrists and would not allow her to get out of bed. We gave her something to eat and started her back on medication. (Malloy, 1998, p. 497)

Discussions and decisions about medication need to include the patient. One patient indicates that:

> ... allowing the ill relative to come to his or her own deci-sion about the necessity of medication in his or her own time can benefit the whole family. As I know from my own experience, once one comes to a decision *oneself* that a given medication or dosage is the best option, medication compliance becomes a dead issue. (Mann, 1999, p. 409)

Neurochemical Mechanisms of Action

All of the first-generation medications have their primary action at the dopamine 2 (D_2) receptor. They are receptor antag-onists, meaning that they act like a defective key in a lock, blocking the receptor so that dopamine cannot bind. This common feature of first-generation antipsychotic drugs led to the theory that schizophrenia was a disease of the dopamine system. Although this theory is now considered overly simplified (because schizophrenia involves more than a single neurotransmitter system), the treatment efficacy of first-generation medications is clearly linked to their ability to bind to the dopamine receptor.

The newer medications also block the dopamine receptor; so why do *these* drugs have reduced movement side effects? One answer may be that the newer medications act on the dopamine receptor in a different fashion. For example, they may block the receptor for shorter periods of time (Kapur, Zipursky, Jones, Shammi et al., 2000)—long enough for a therapeutic effect but not long enough to cause movement side effects. Another difference is that the newer medications act on many different receptors in addition to the D_2 receptor. In particular, all of them block the serotonin receptors (including the serotonin 2_A receptor subtype). There is considerable speculation among scientists that the combination of efficacy and reduced side effects of newer medications depends on the balance of the actions at the dopamine and serotonin receptors. It is possible that the actions at the serotonin receptor are especially important for some of the other characteristics of newer medications, such as their effects on neurocognition.

Interventions for Neurocognitive Deficits

Given the centrality of neurocognitive deficits to schizophrenia (chapter 4), as well as their relationships to outcome (chapter 7), it is natural to wonder whether neurocognitive deficits should become targets of treatment themselves. Once a patient is clinically stabilized so that the psychotic symptoms are managed, it is reasonable to focus on remaining deficits, especially ones that may prevent that individual from fully re-engaging in community activities. Trying to find interventions for the neurocognitive deficits of schizophrenia is a recent endeavor, but during the last decade, this research area has taken off and become something of a preoccupation. In general, there are two ways to bring about improvement in neurocognitive deficits: through pharmacological interventions and through nonpharmacological means such as cognitive retraining.

Psychopharmacological Interventions

Old versus new antipsychotic medications. There were two general impressions about the neurocognitive effects of the first-generation antipsychotic medications. One was that these drugs' profound beneficial effect on symptoms would act like a rising tide to improve all types of deficits, including those of neurocognition. The second impression was that the drugs were actually *causing* the neurocognitive deficits because of their sedating properties. As it turns out, both of these impressions are wrong. A perusal of various neurocognitive domains, including abstraction and problem solving, learning and memory, neuromotor abilities, visuospatial abilities, and verbal abilities, reveals that, with few exceptions, first-generation antipsychotic medications have minimal effects on neurocognition (Cassens, Inglis, Appelbaum, & Gutheil, 1990; Cornblatt et al., 1997). Those few exceptions can include beneficial effects on vigilance as measured with the Continuous Performance Test (CPT) (Earle-Boyer, Serper, Davidson, & Harvey, 1991; Latz & Kornetsky, 1965; Orzack, Kornetsky, & Freeman, 1967; Spohn, Lacoursiere, Thompson, & Coyne, 1977) and backward masking (Braff & Saccuzzo, 1982). But other areas of neurocognition do not show consistent effects of antipsychotic medications, despite the major impact these drugs have on psychotic symptoms. This incongruence between clinical and neurocognitive treatment-effects gives additional support for the relative independence of neurocognitive performance and psychotic symptoms that was mentioned in chapter 4.

Although first-generation antipsychotic medications do not appear to impair neurocognitive abilities directly, they may do so indirectly. As mentioned, the movement side effects associated with these antipsychotic medications are often treated with drugs that block the acetylcholine receptor. These anticholinergic drugs take a toll on certain neurocognitive abilities, particularly components of memory (Spohn & Strauss, 1989). They seem to be especially disruptive for aspects of secondary (longer-term) verbal memory, and less for immediate or working memory (Drachman & Leavitt, 1974; Sweeney, Keilp, Haas, Hill, & Weiden, 1991). If drugs that reduce acetylcholine disrupt memory, then drugs that increase acetylcholine may help memory. Indeed, it is no accident that the only drugs currently approved for use with dementia, such as Alzheimer's Disease, are designed to increase acetylcholine activity (Davis & Powchik, 1995).

In contrast to the first generation of medications, the neurocognitive effects of the newer atypical antipsychotic agents appear more promising (see reviews in Keefe, Silva, Perkins, & Lieberman, 1999; Meltzer & McGurk, 1999). Information on this topic has emerged in the sequence that the drugs were introduced (see Table 6.1). At this time, published research on the neurocognitive effects of clozapine, risperidone, and olanzapine exists, and there are ongoing studies for all of the new drugs, including quetiapine and ziprasidone. A cautionary note, however: Most of the studies on these new drugs have used methods that are less than ideal (e.g., small sample sizes, lack of optimal comparison groups, or groups that were not randomly assigned to medication). Nonetheless, the conclusions are inescapable.

Clozapine was the first of the newer antipsychotic medications to be approved in the United States, and the first to be examined for its neurocognitive effects. Perhaps the most consistent finding was that, compared to first-generation medications, clozapine improved verbal fluency (Buchanan, Holstein, & Breier, 1994; Hagger et al., 1993; Hoff et al., 1996). Verbal fluency refers to our ability to generate words that begin with a certain letter or belong to a certain category. For example, participants could be asked to generate all of the words they can think of that begin with the letter "A," or all of the animals they can think of, in a one-minute period. Clozapine also seemed to improve motor speed. Despite these neurocognitive advantages, some studies showed that clozapine treatment had short-term detrimental effects on visual memory and verbal working memory (Hagger et al., 1993; Hoff et al., 1996).

Our laboratory explored the neurocognitive effects of risperidone, the second of the approved newer medications. Patients were randomly assigned to a first-generation drug (haloperidol) or to risperidone. Treatment with risperidone yielded improvements on tasks of immediate memory (similar to remembering a telephone number) and secondary verbal memory (remembering lists of words) (Green, Marshall, et al., 1997; Kern et al., 1999). Unlike the findings from clozapine, risperidone did not seem to improve verbal fluency, and it did not appear to present any short-term detrimental effects on memory.

Findings on the neurocognitive effects of olanzapine are emerging. The most comprehensive published study to date comes from the manufacturer of olanzapine. It shows neurocognitive benefit over a first-generation drug, and even some benefits over risperidone in neurocognitive areas, including immediate memory and motor skills (Purdon et al., 2000). Preliminary findings from the companies that make the other two newer medications, quetiapine and ziprasidone, also indicate neurocognitive advantages for these drugs, at least compared with first-generation drugs.

Overall, there is a "generation gap" between the new and old medications. The new-generation medications provide neurocognitive benefits when compared to the first-generation medications. The neurocognitive benefit of the newer medications may be related to the fact that all of the newer medications block both the D_2 and the serotonin receptors. Perhaps there is something about the balance of serotonin and dopamine activity that is good for neurocognition. Although the newer medications are better for neurocognition, they do not usually bring performance up to normal levels. In our work with very chronic patients, we find that the improvement makes up about half of the difference between initial patient performance and normal levels. Patients frequently notice the differences in movement side effects between the old and new medications. However, subjective aspects of neurocognition are rarely studied, and it is not known if patients perceive the neurocognitive differences between types of medication.

The neurocognitive results from new-generation medications are remarkable for two reasons. One is that, for the first time, the medications of schizophrenia are acting on a domain of illness that is separate from and independent of clinical symptoms. Second, as we see in the next section, the neurocognitive benefits of these drugs are serendipitous.

Novel approaches for drug treatments. The new-generation medications were not developed as treatments for neurocognition, and they were not evaluated with neurocognition in mind. If these medications are good for neurocognition, as they appear to be, then it is a fortunate accident. Scientists can now capitalize on this accident and speculate on how the new generation of medications convey this benefit.

Once an effective drug is found, scientists try to discover the neurochemical properties that make it a good drug. This information leads to theories about the neurotransmitter systems (such as dopamine and serotonin) that are critical for the disorder. But consider for a moment what is wrong with this process—it works backwards. Wouldn't it make more sense if developments in neuroscience led to the discoveries of new medications, instead of the other way around? And wouldn't it be better if we first decided what neurochemical processes were responsible for a certain neurocognitive deficit in schizophrenia and then tried to influence them with medications? This is just beginning to occur, and it requires thinking "outside the box."

In a promising new line of investigation, scientists have started to examine a completely different neurotransmitter system. Glutamate is the most common neurotransmitter in the brain, and its role in schizophrenia is just now being understood (Olney & Farber, 1995). One of the reasons for interest in this receptor is that when one type of glutamate receptor (the NMDA subtype) is blocked in normal controls, they show subtle clinical signs and neurocognitive deficits similar to those seen in schizophrenia (Krystal et al., 1994; Malhotra et al., 1996).

New drugs are being tested that act on the NMDA glutamate receptor. These experiments are trying to determine whether drugs that affect the glutamate system can improve neurocognitive deficits and negative symptoms, the features of schizophrenia that are more difficult to treat. These new drugs (e.g., D-cycloserine, and D-serine) are used as adjunctive medications, meaning that they are taken in addition to, not instead of, antipsychotic medications. The very few studies so far suggest that negative symptoms and neurocognition sometimes improve with these types of drugs (Goff, Tsai, Manoach, & Coyle, 1995; Tsai, Yang, Chung, Lange, & Coyle, 1998).

What is notable about these studies is how they stem directly from advances in the neuroscience of schizophrenia. We are approaching a new era, in which treatment developments will grow out of knowledge about the neural processes that underlie the signs and symptoms of schizophrenia. The treatment targets in these studies extend far beyond positive psychotic symptoms and include neurocognitive deficits and negative symptoms. If these studies of adjunctive agents show reliable improvement in neurocognition in schizophrenia, it may become routine for schizophrenic patients to take separate types of medications, one for psychotic symptoms and another for neurocognitive deficits (Davidson & Keefe, 1995). It should not come as a surprise if a disease this complex turns out to require more than one treatment.

Cognitive rehabilitation. Can we train patients to have better neurocognition? Can neurocognition in schizophrenia be taught and learned, like history or astronomy; is it something that can be exercised, like a tennis serve; or is it more like intelligence, which we expect patients to carry with them, largely unchanged, for the rest of their lives? There are several studies showing that patients can improve their performance on neurocognitive measures with training exercises. For example, patients sometimes show gains on tests of card sorting (Wisconsin Card Sorting Test) and vigilance (Continuous Performance Test) (Green, 1993; Green, Satz, Ganzell, & Vaclav, 1992; Medalia, Aluma, Tryon, & Merriam, 1998). Even simple training techniques such as coaching and reinforcement can yield short-term gains. However, changing patients' performance on a test is a hollow victory if the gains are short-lived and do not make a difference in their daily lives. Efforts are underway to find training techniques that have longer lasting effects. It appears that extensive practice, as in any other type of training, increases the longevity of the effects (Wexler et al., 1997). Also, specialized techniques designed to reduce the number of errors during training appear to produce more durable effects (Kern, Wallace, Hellman, Womack, & Green, 1996). So, if techniques are used that produce reasonably long-lasting effects (for weeks or months), do they really benefit the patients? In other words, do the effects of training "generalize" to the daily lives of patients?

The simple answer is that we are not yet sure how well these techniques generalize. Sometimes the results do not even generalize from one neurocognitive task to a similar one (Benedict et al., 1994). But recent reports provide a basis for optimism. For example, training-related changes in mental flexibility were related to improvement in social functioning in a relatively short (8-week) training trial (Wykes, Reeder, Corner, Williams, & Everitt, 1999). In another project, training on card sorting yielded improved social competence, and gains in verbal memory were linked to increased psychosocial skill acquisition over a 6-month intervention (Spaulding et al., 1999). These studies are encouraging but still preliminary. They suggest that if we can develop potent neurocognitive retraining techniques, the effects may extend to improved functional outcome. The hope is to develop neurocognitive training techniques with long coattails.

These nonpharmacological approaches for neurocognitive deficits are often called "neurocognitive rehabilitation," or "cognitive remediation," terms that are sometimes confused with "cognitive behavioral therapy" for schizophrenia. Although the terms sound alike, the goals are very different. Cognitive behavioral therapy for schizophrenia uses psychotherapeutic approaches to treat the symptoms of schizophrenia and the distress that they cause. The term "cognitive" is used because the therapy requires patients to alter their beliefs, views, and assumptions about symptoms—essentially to shift their attitude

(Beck, Rush, Shaw, & Emery, 1979; Garety, Fowler, & Kuipers, 2000). For example, a suspicious patient who believes that his house is bugged and that he is being followed by the CIA would first work with the therapist to minimize the distress caused by his beliefs. In addition, the therapist would encourage him to generate alternative explanations for the experiences and to view his delusional beliefs as "hypotheses" that can be systematically tested and disproven. This form of therapy seems to work well for patients who do not have full conviction in their delusions. Note the targets of this form of therapy are the symptoms of the illness (and related discomfort), whereas in cognitive retraining the focus is on the neurocognitive deficits.

Interventions for Functional Outcome

Community Care

Coupled with the exodus of patients from the state hospitals to the community in the 1960s went an increased need for community-based mental health services. Unfortunately, adequate community support for chronic patients was often lacking, and many fell through the rather porous safety net. Community services were limited and often difficult to access, even though they were located closer to patients. This problem was especially pronounced for chronic patients who had been hospitalized over long periods of time and did not have the skills (and/or inclination) to navigate the complex mental health system. Even today it is clear that individuals dropped by the community mental health system fill the ranks of the homeless and swell the prison census.

In response to the needs of chronic patients in the community, several community care models were created. Among the most successful are those based on "assertive community treatment," or ACT (Stein & Test, 1980). Their goal is to be readily available so that patients know support can be easily accessed. Patients in these programs learn that no question is too minor, and no time is too late. ACT services are delivered by a treatment team usually consisting of a psychiatrist, a nurse, and case managers. The programs have several features, including a relatively small number of patients for each staff member (about 10 to 1), services that are provided in the community (e.g., the patient's home) instead of in an office, shared caseloads so patients can see other members of the treatment team, 24-hour coverage, and time-unlimited service (Mueser, Bond, Drake, & Resnick, 1998).

Do the ACT programs work? It depends on the goal. These programs are very good at keeping patients out of the hospital and increasing the stability of housing arrangements. They are sometimes helpful for reducing symptoms, probably because patients are less likely to stop taking their medication. By themselves, however, these programs do not offer benefits for social adjustment (i.e., social relationships, role functioning, and social networks) or vocational outcome (Mueser et al., 1998). This lack of success with social and vocational outcome should not come as a surprise, since the ACT programs do not offer training specifically for these purposes. In the absence of training, many chronic patients, especially those who have spent long periods of time in the hospital, do not have the necessary skills for improving social adjustment. To impart these skills, another type of intervention is needed—social skills training.

Social Skills Training

Suppose you have a brother with schizophrenia who lives alone in an apartment and has few friends. He complains of being socially isolated, of going days without talking to anyone. In an effort to be helpful, you make an innocent suggestion that he walk down to the local coffee shop, buy a cup of coffee, and have a simple conversation with a person sitting there. After all, how difficult can that be? The answer is, nearly impossible if one does not have the requisite skills. Everything from preparing a meal and managing finances to communicating with a psychiatrist about medication side effects requires psychosocial skills that many patients are lacking. Some patients had the skills before they became ill, others never really had them.

How does one train patients in the use of such skills? If you are a behaviorist, you would use behavioral principals such as reinforcing desired behaviors and ignoring nondesired behaviors. In the 1960s and 1970s, a time of high confidence in behavioral interventions for all types of problems, behaviorism swept into psychiatric inpatient units in the form of "token economies" (Paul & Lentz, 1977). These were essentially miniature market economies in which patients could earn tokens for targeted behaviors such as making their beds, cleaning up after their meals, and actively participating in unit activities. The patients could redeem the tokens for items and privileges that they really wanted (e.g., snacks, music, the privilege to walk on grounds without supervision). These programs had their limitations: They required heavy time investments from staff. In addition, it took time for patients to become accustomed to them. For these reasons, it was much more difficult to maintain these programs when patients had short-term hospital stays and when they re-entered the community. Nonetheless, these token economies constituted a shift in thinking about chronic schizophrenic patients; the emphasis shifted to training and reinforcing important life skills.

Modern social skills training programs are the legacy of these early token economies. Although social skills training is considered a form of therapy, it bears no resemblance to stereotyped notions of therapy. There is no lying on the couch, no long pauses, and no talking about one's childhood. It is more like dance lessons. The patients learn simple steps and gradually combine the simple behaviors into more complex ones.

In social skills training, a particular group of skills is selected; these could include skills necessary for managing symptoms, for community re-entry, or for starting and maintaining conversations. Complex behaviors are broken down into their elements. For example, training on conversational skills would start with simpler components (maintaining eye contact, taking turns in speaking, maintaining proper voice volume, selecting topics, and ending the conversation on a positive note) before putting them all together in role-play exercises. The trainers use a range of techniques, including teaching, demonstrating the desired behavior, coaching the patient during role-plays of desired behavior, giving strong verbal encouragement, and assigning homework (Heinssen, Liberman, & Kopelowicz, 2000). Target behaviors are "shaped," meaning that initial behaviors, even if not perfect, are reinforced, as long as they represent steps in the right direction. The behaviors must progressively resemble the desired behavior to be reinforced, until finally, only the desired behavior is reinforced.

Schizophrenic patients can learn a wide range of skills, from basic behaviors to more complex ones such as assertiveness and self-management of medications (Penn & Mueser, 1996). The training occurs in small groups of 4 to 8 patients and tends to be repetitive to increase the chances that the information will be retained by patients who have memory deficits. The programs can last for months and are designed for both inpatients and outpatients. Some patients can demonstrate the skills when prompted months after the training. Even though patients know how to use the skills when prompted, it is still not clear whether they actually use them spontaneously in their daily lives. Social skills training tends to yield better social adjustment for patients. But social skills training alone does not appear to reduce rates of relapse and rehospitalization.

Social skills training and community care programs such as ACT can be combined. The approaches are complementary: Social skills training provides the prerequisites for functional outcome in the community; ACT helps to keep the patients in the community and out of the hospital. The difficulty is often getting access to either type of program. Although implementation of these types of programs is increasing dramatically, their availability is limited. This may be due to the laws of the marketplace: The same kind of profit motive for introducing and disseminating new drugs does not exist for psychosocial treatments (Lehman, 2000).

Interventions in the Family Context

All of the treatments discussed so far were for the individual patient. The patients themselves take the medications, participate in the skills training, or see the case manager. Schizophrenia, however, touches everyone in the family. Although some patients are alienated from their families, many live with them or at least have ongoing contact. So, it is no surprise that interventions have evolved within the family context.

Several related approaches to psychosocial interventions are grouped under the label "family psychoeducation," which are programs that offer practical and emotional support, crisis management, information about mental illness, and help with problem solving (Dixon, Adams, & Luckstead, 2000; Penn & Mueser, 1996). Current programs do not assume that family interactions are responsible for the illness, and they avoid blaming the family for the patient's illness. This sensitivity stems from the history of family studies in schizophrenia, which started by examining the role of family communications.

Studies of "expressed emotion," which originated in the United Kingdom in the early 1970s and then spread to the United States, indicated that patients were more likely to relapse if they lived with family members who demonstrated certain qualities in their communications with or about the patient (e.g., critical, hostile, or emotionally overinvolved). This became a controversial area for reasons that have little to do with science. Family members understandably perceived these studies as placing some "blame" on their shoulders. Scientists, just as understandably, did not think they were blaming anyone, but instead were simply trying to find predictors of relapse. In fact, studies of expressed emotion were ambiguous about cause (a chicken and egg situation) because they could not determine if these qualities in family members were long-standing, or if they were a reaction to the patient's illness. Nonetheless, this area launched the initial attempts at family intervention that were designed to help families with high expressed emotion learn to communicate with lower expressed emotion (i.e., reduced hostility). This type of therapy reduced relapses and served as a starting point for more current comprehensive family psychoeducation programs (Leff, Kuipers, Berkowitz, & Sturgeon, 1985).

Modern family interventions are designed for all families, not only those with high expressed emotion. One of the most important goals of these programs is to provide education about illness. In a highly misunderstood disorder such as schizophrenia, education *is* intervention. Many families know little about the illness and are unsure what to expect. Sometimes family members are initially reluctant to admit that the patient even has the condition. With education programs, the families learn about the importance of taking medications, managing stress, monitoring early warning signs of relapse, identifying side effects, and setting realistic expectations for the future. Families can become an invaluable treatment resource for the patient. In this personal account, the daughter of a mother with schizophrenia describes the importance of family psychoeducation.

> In 1989, my older sister and I joined Mom in her attempts to learn more about managing symptoms of her illness. Mom's caseworkers met with us every 6 to 8 weeks for over 8 years. Mom, who had never been able to admit she had an illness, now told us that she did not want to die a psychotic. This was one of the many positive steps that we have observed in her recovery. Over the years, other family members have joined our group. . . . With the help of the treatment team, we can now respond *effectively* to Mom's symptoms and identify stress-producing situations that, if left unaddressed, can lead to episodes of hospitalization. With Mom's help we have identified the different stages of her illness. In the first stage we listed withdrawal, confusion, depression, and sleeping disorder. Fifteen years ago when Mom reported her symptoms to me, I just told her everything would be okay. Today we respond immediately. For 8 years she has maintained a low dosage of medications, with increases during times of stress. (Sundquist, 1999, p. 620)

In addition to enlisting the family's help as therapeutic agents, these programs also deal directly with the stresses that schizophrenia imposes. Few illnesses place stress and burden on the family like schizophrenia. As mentioned in chapter 1, it is an illness that unfortunately still carries stigma. In addition, there is the inevitable disruption caused by relapses and hospitalization. The first episode of illness is especially confusing for families. A son or daughter who was once warm and loving becomes remote and unpredictable. The illness is all too often associated with additional problems such as drug abuse, homelessness, and suicide. Helping families to cope with this type of stress, often in groups of multiple families, is a key goal of family interventions. Helping families to know what to expect from the illness is another. One of the most common misunderstandings is to expect the illness to go away when the psychotic symptoms do. Even after psychosis has resolved, the negative symptoms make it difficult to reestablish a sense of interpersonal connectedness, and, as we will see, neurocognitive deficits and other lingering problems make it difficult to resume community functioning.

Chapter Seven

Outcome in Schizophrenia

Overcoming Disability

What's the magic cure? How did I go from being an angry, distrusting, "treatment-resistant schizophrenic" to a woman entering graduate school, who lives with schizophrenia? There's no magic cure. All I offer to my fellow travelers is this: Be patient with yourself. Take time to have fun. Work hard. Be passionate. Be willing to trust yourself and others. Take your meds.

(Greenblat, 2000, p. 245)

Outcome in schizophrenia is highly variable. Whereas some individuals establish full and productive lives, many others do not. Diseases have a certain prognosis—a sense of what to expect for the average patient. When someone receives a diagnosis of schizophrenia, patients and families immediately want to know what the future will bring. Is schizophrenia closer to a life sentence, or more like a temporary setback? No simple answer exists, partly because there are several different categories of outcome, as well as tremendous differences from person to person within the outcome categories. In the previous chapter, we discussed the introduction of antipsychotic medications and spoke with a warranted enthusiasm about these medications. What difference have these medications made for outcome in schizophrenia? Much less than one would think.

Figure 7.1 shows a summary of long-term outcome studies in schizophrenia across the twentieth century (Hegarty, Baldessarini, Tohen, Waternaux, & Oepen, 1994). The bars show the percentage of patients who were rated as improved at follow-up for studies published in different decades. Follow-up periods were, on average, about 5 years. The definitions of outcome differed across time and across studies, but the intention of figure 7.1 was to represent the percentages of patients who were improved on both symptomatic and functional outcomes. Despite these different ways to measure outcome, as well as different ways to diagnose schizophrenia, the results are surprisingly consistent across the century. On average, about 40 percent of the patients showed improvement. The introduction of antipsychotic medications in the 1950s may have resulted in some gains in outcome in the 1960s and 1970s, but these gains are faint in comparison to the degree of symptom management that was achieved during this period. In addition, the gains started to erode in the 1980s and 1990s (possibly due to changes in diagnostic criteria). This figure illustrates that even with effective medications schizophrenia remains a remarkably disabling illness. If our treatments are so good, why are the outcomes so often bad? The resolution lies in the fact that the medications (at least the first-generation medications) work mainly on symptoms, and symptoms account for only one type of outcome in schizophrenia.

Long-Term Outcome in Schizophrenia

One source of information on the course of schizophrenia comes from a group of patients in Vermont who were followed by Courtenay Harding and colleagues (Harding, Brooks, Ashikaga, Strauss, & Breier, 1987). These were patients who were admitted to Vermont State Hospital in the 1950s and reassessed in the early 1980s. Results from this project were reasonably optimistic: About a third of the sample had recovered from their symptoms, and about another third had shown symptomatic improvement but not full recovery. Unlike Kraepelin's original

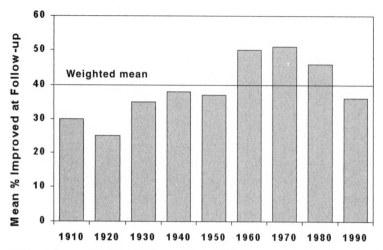

Figure 7.1 ▪ *Patient improvement at follow-up across the twentieth century. This figure shows the percent of patients who showed good outcome at follow-up during each decade of the twentieth century. From* The American Journal of Psychiatry, 151, *p. 1412. Copyright 1994, the American Psychiatric Association. Reprinted by permission.*

idea that schizophrenia had mainly a deteriorating course and predominantly poor prognosis, this follow-up study suggested that outcome in schizophrenia can be positive. Nonetheless, the results varied widely from patient to patient, as illustrated by these two case studies (Harding, 1988).

K. U.—Poor Outcome Patient

At age 68, K. U. is a slender man. . . . He was born in 1912 and was the middle brother of two sisters. He had an unremarkable childhood and attended church school until the eighth grade. . . . His sister described him as a steady, and reliable worker. "In fact," she said, "he led an average, energetic, happy life before his illness." Although shy, K. U. had many close friends and belonged to an orchestra where he played violin and piano. In his early twenties, he liked one girl very much but "broke off with her because she drank." After the relationship dissolved, he withdrew from socializing, quit playing music, stopped working, and claimed that electricity was "put in him at night and would not let him sleep."

In 1935, at age 23, he was admitted to Vermont State Hospital, 3 months after the relationship ended. He was quiet and restless, with poor stream of thought and difficulty speaking. His auditory hallucinations were both pleasant and harsh as well as constant. . . . He was discharged home within 8 months. . . . He had a second admission in 1949 for 2 months with a similar symptom profile. In 1950 he began a 12-year stint in his index hospitalization at the State hospital. He had not worked since his discharge the year before. He had spent his days lying around, undressed, pacing by the hour in his room. In his self-imposed seclusion, he did not read, talk, or participate. His voice was low, flat, and expressionless, and he only spoke when spoken to. He did not eat except to pick at food. . . .

This behavior abated very slowly. He entered the rehabilitation program in 1958. He would clean the barn 7 days a week, leaving early in the morning and returning to the hospital to sleep, avoiding any contact. The rehabilitation team felt he "hid behind the job," and it took them a year to get him out of the barn and into other more sociable jobs. He was described as quiet, taciturn, and free of hallucinations and delusions. He was released to the halfway house in 1961.

By 1978 he was described as quite paranoid, ritualistic, apprehensive, reclusive, cloistered and phobic. He stayed up all night and slept all day. Mr. U. always opened and shut doors six times when entering or leaving the room as well as turning on and off lights repeatedly. He had been mute for 2 years. He had not been out of the house in 5 years nor seen any clinician. He ate by himself and spent considerable time facing the wall. He refused baths, shaving, or haircuts. The police brought him to the hospital for his fourth admission in September 1978. Upon admission, he requested a haircut and shave. However, he insisted that he use his shirt-sleeves to grasp doorknobs, chairs, or eating utensils instead of his fingers. . . . He was discharged to home; the community mental health center for fluphenazine decanoate 25 mg q 3 weeks, benztropine 2 mg a day; and a day treatment program.

In 1980, follow-up interviews were conducted. The rater found a tidy Vermont farmhouse full of extended family members and the father's sculptures. Mr. U.'s sisters and their daughters spoke in grumpy, loud, hostile, and argumentative voices. . . . He was unemployed with a guardian managing his money, which came from public funding. He continued with the day program and medication regimen. He had minimal socializing and was primarily dependent on his family, had adequate social supports, and relied on casual contacts for companionship. He appeared reasonably neat, clean, and appropriate. He displayed minimal sense of humor. Life was serious business. The community mental health center played the major role in his social life.

N. H.—Patient with Long-Term Improvement

The patient was one of seven children, three brothers and three sisters. . . . She reportedly got along well with everyone but had a tendency to be stubborn and demanding with her family. . . .

She divorced her second husband in 1946 after he had been absent from the home for approximately 5 years. After this divorce, the patient reportedly became "boy crazy" and wanted children badly. She became involved in a number of different relationships, many of which were abusive and self-destructive. It appears from the record, that the patient was very needy and made very quick and intense attachments to men whom she barely knew. Ultimately, the patient reported that she was pregnant from one of these relationships. It was never clear whether this "pregnancy" was a real or imagined event. . . .

At Mrs. H.'s first hospitalization [February 1954, at age 40], she was admitted looking disheveled and furtive. Her hair was prematurely gray. She described years of visual and auditory hallucinations. In addition to her "phantom pregnancy" 4 years earlier, she felt she now was carrying twins even in the face of a very heavy menstrual flow. She continued to be abrasive to parents and difficult to control. She was friendly and cooperative, making no objection to admission, but certain her sister had engineered it out of jealousy. Before admission, she was washing her face with milk, smearing butter in her hair, and repeating the Lord's Prayer all day long. She began calling doctors because she felt her body and face were shrinking. She began to lose weight, refusing to eat because she thought her parents were poisoning her food. After the first year, she became so violent and assaultive that she was sent to a maximum security ward for several months. She gradually regained her composure, improved her behavior, and was released from the hospital to her family in an improved state after the second year.

In a year, at age 43, she returned for her index hospitalization with the same paranoid delusions as before. She believed she was pregnant and her relatives wanted to get rid of her. Although quiet and cooperative, able to eat and sleep well, she displayed silly and inappropriate affect, smiling and giggling without apparent cause. She was also confused, highly illogical, irrelevant, and incoherent. . . . She then went through several episodes of being bellicose and belligerent, once again regaining her aplomb and leaving the hospital in an improved state in 1958.

She returned for her third admission in 1960, having been sleepless, refusing medication, and throwing a plate at her mother. She talked incessantly about babies and children. She claimed to be President Eisenhower's nurse and married to certain officials and doctors. Over the next 10 years, she was rehospitalized four more times for periods of 1 to 2 months each. Over the years, N. H. became very independent, managing her own apartment and her medication. She began to participate in her local community mental health center programs. She approached life with her old sense of humor.

At follow-up, N. H. was 67 years old. Her family, which had been so problematic to her in the past, was now her source of caring and belonging. She was living with her sister in an apartment. There were no signs of symptoms, and it was difficult to guess that she had spent so many years at the hospital. Her recent involvement with the local community mental health center consisted of medication checks every 3 months. She was on a low dose of trifluoperazine. Overall, she seemed quite satisfied with her life and felt it had improved a great deal over the years.

These two cases provide some concrete examples of good versus poor outcome in schizophrenia. Based on studies from the past two decades, about half of the patients with schizophrenia can be considered to have a poor outcome (Moller & Von Zerssen, 1995). So what factors can account for the differences in outcome between patients like K. U. and N. H.? They both received similar types of treatments from the same hospital. If we met them early in their illness, would we notice something that would tell us what to expect? Perhaps there are tests we could give that would help to predict outcome. Recent research has uncovered several determinants of outcome in schizophrenia. While there is no such thing as perfect prediction (for this or any other illness), scientists are starting to understand the building blocks for good outcome and to make better predictions. The first task is to realize that outcome is not a simple or unitary concept in schizophrenia; there are several different types.

Outcome may look reasonably good for clinical symptoms alone, but not for other aspects such as social and occupational functioning. For example, in Iceland, all of the patients who experienced a first episode of schizophrenia from 1966–67 were followed for 20 years (Helgason, 1990). In terms of clinical symptoms, 4 percent were in complete remission and 29 percent had achieved reasonably good symptom outcome (remission or only minor symptoms). These indications of symptomatic improvement were moderately encouraging, but other indications of outcome were highly concerning. Twenty-two percent had died (twice the national average) and 9 percent had committed suicide (twenty times the national average). About half had never married, and almost the entire sample (95 percent) had impaired social relationships at follow-up.

Domains of Outcome

To illustrate why it is important to distinguish among types of outcome in schizophrenia, try a thought experiment. Imagine a community in which psychotic symptoms are relatively common. Many of the inhabitants of this community experience auditory hallucinations, including command hallucinations, in which they hear voices telling them to do something. They also have delusions of reference, that is, objects and events have special meaning for them. In this particular community, these symptoms are not seen as aberrant; on the contrary, they are seen as special. How would one recognize schizophrenia in this community? Does it have something to do with the amount of symptoms? Does it have to do with the types of symptoms? Or does it have to do with something entirely separate from the psychotic symptoms? The answer is the latter.

There is such a community; at least we have a description of such a community. It is detailed in the Old Testament. Hearing voices was fairly common, and events and objects often took on a special significance. In contrast, schizophrenia-like insanity is rarely described. When insanity is described in the Old Testament, it always has one feature: It is characterized by *functional* impairment. One compelling description of insanity occurs in the Book of Daniel. The King of Babylon, Nebuchadnezzar, has a disturbing dream about a great tree that provided fruit and shade for all, until it was suddenly cut down. Daniel interpreted the cutting of the great tree to mean that the king would fall into madness and be cast out to live among the animals. In a particularly revealing detail, the stump of the tree is left in a band of metal, much like a shackle for the insane:

> Nevertheless leave the stump of its roots in the earth,
> Even in a band of iron and brass, in the tender grass of the field;
> And let it be wet with the dew of heaven,
> And let this portion be with the beasts in the grass of earth
> —Daniel 4:12

Later, Daniel's interpretation comes to pass:

> The same hour was the thing fulfilled upon Nebuchadnezzar; and he was driven from men, and did eat grass as oxen, and his body was wet with the dew of heaven, till his hair was grown like eagles' feathers, and his nails like birds' claws.
> —Daniel 4:30

The king proved to be a good outcome patient, and after a period of time, he recovered ("mine understanding returned to me") and resumed his role on the throne. This biblical story illustrates that psychotic symptoms alone do not make a diagnosis, and it is critical to consider clinical and functional outcome separately in schizophrenia.

Functional Outcome: Social, Vocational, and Independent Living

Functional outcome includes a broad range of activities, including social, vocational, and independent living. Problems in these areas are absolutely central to schizophrenia. In fact, functional impairment is the only illness feature that is shared by everyone with a diagnosis of schizophrenia. Patients are often socially awkward, frequently emotionally distant from family and friends, and rarely employed. Frequently, the social difficulties begin before the onset of psychotic symptoms and before the illness is diagnosed. These difficulties are part of early indications of schizophrenia, called the prodrome.

> [I]n junior high I became more friendly and outgoing. During this time, I was a cheerleader and active in student government, of which I was elected president. Starting in my freshman year of high school I was on the varsity tennis team. Then, in my sophomore year, I withdrew from the cheerleaders' squad, not wanting to be in the spotlight. I became very introverted, read a lot of books, and wrote poetry and prose most of the time. I had few friends, and except for being on the tennis team, I withdrew socially. I had more crying spells, cut my wrists with razor blades, and overdosed on aspirin. My parents sent me to a psychiatric nurse for counseling. She and the consulting psychiatrist did not suspect schizophrenia at that time. (Murphy, 1997, p. 541)

The prodromal period is one of great confusion for the affected individuals, the families, and clinicians. In the midst of the prodrome described above, it would have been nearly impossible to determine if the social withdrawal was part of the prodrome for schizophrenia, a sign of depression, or a temporary adjustment disorder of adolescence. The prodromal period is typically defined in retrospect, after the onset of the psychotic symptoms. The individual who wrote the personal account above started to have psychotic symptoms as a young adult. The psychotic symptoms responded well to treatment; however, despite successful symptom management, she could not maintain employment.

> It is true that, even though I consider myself methodical in nature, my life had been very chaotic up until 1994. I went

through 20 paid jobs and 6 volunteer positions. The longest I was able to stay with a paid job was 18 months, and it was only part-time. (Murphy, 1997, p. 542)

Few schizophrenic patients go on to become employed; the precise numbers range from 7 to 53 percent (Cook & Razzano, 2000). The large range in the percentages is partly due to differences in unemployment rates across regions and time. In addition, the definition of employment can sometimes mean unpaid work in the home. A much smaller number of individuals with schizophrenia go on to have "competitive" employment, meaning that the job was obtained through a normal application process and not part of a sheltered work program. Estimates of competitive employment in schizophrenia range from 10 to 20 percent (McGlashan, 1988). Getting a job is only part of the challenge; maintaining one is the other. It is common for patients who are placed in jobs to experience unsatisfactory job terminations.

Work, social interactions, and college classes present unique challenges for persons with schizophrenia. Even when individuals with schizophrenia are able to manage these challenges successfully, it comes only with great effort, as described next:

College had been an on-and-off 14-year struggle. Studying was not easy. Because of poor concentration, I had to re-read countless sentences and settle for low grades on in-class exams. In the past, I had to withdraw from several sessions because the stress was too much. . . . My work and educational experiences illustrate just how hard I had to work to stand on a level playing field with "normal" people. It is often difficult not to compare myself to others and feel discouraged. (Dykstra, 1997, p. 698)

Sometimes it takes a major success to reveal a prominent failure. Partly due to the progress in treating clinical symptoms, the lack of improvement in social contacts, work, school, and independent living have come into sharper focus. These features constitute the disability of schizophrenia. For many years, clinical and functional outcomes were seen as interdependent. On the contrary, clinical outcome is simply different.

Clinical Outcome

Clinical outcome is based on the presence or absence of clinical symptoms (described in chapter 1), including positive, disorganized, and negative symptoms. Positive symptoms are always evaluated for clinical outcome, and more recent studies also consider the presence of negative symptoms. Although some patients have a complete remission of symptoms, it is more common for patients to achieve partial remission in which toned-down versions of symptoms remain. Full conviction in a delusion may give way to a "partial" delusion. For example, instead of being sure that one's food has been poisoned, a person may occasionally wonder about the possibility. Likewise, full auditory hallucinations that occur in the absence of any sounds may subside to periodic illusions in which the person thinks voices may be present, but only in the presence of other noises. Although these milder symptoms do not sound enjoyable to a non-ill person, they are not necessarily disruptive to functioning, nor necessarily problematic for the individual. It is becoming increasingly clear that a good outcome does not require a complete absence of symptoms.

The early conceptualization of schizophrenia (most notably by Kraepelin) was pessimistic and emphasized the poor course and outcome over time. The expectation was that the older the patient, the more severe the illness. In contrast, modern follow-up studies show that deteriorating clinical course is the exception, not the rule. Part of the credit goes to improved treatments, including antipsychotic medications. Aside from advances in clinical management, it appears that symptoms follow a natural course—they become progressively worse on average for the first 5 to 10 years of the illness, but they tend to plateau and often mellow with age (McGlashan, 1988), although some follow-up studies identify a subgroup of patients with a progressive deteriorating course (Ciompi, 1980). In addition, some patients show a decline in functional outcome and/or neurocognitive abilities in later life (e.g., beyond the age of 65) (Harvey, Parrella, White, Mohs, & Davis, 1999). Nonetheless, only a minority of patients show a clear progressive increase in clinical symptoms across the life span.

Subjective Satisfaction

There can be large differences between the outcome that a person attains, and how they feel about it. In other words, there is a discrepancy between objective and subjective outcome. John Brekke and his colleagues have shown that outcome in schizophrenia can be separated into three distinct domains: functional, clinical, and subjective (Brekke, Levin, Wolkon, Sobel, & Slade, 1993). As mentioned above, clinical and functional outcome are independent forms of outcome. Similarly, subjective outcome is negligibly related to functional outcome, and these two types of outcome do not change together over time. Thus, a patient with schizophrenia may, over the course of a year, increase the amount of time spent with friends, increase contact with family, and live more independently—but *not necessarily feel any better* about these changes.

To understand this seeming contradiction, think about increases in your own "functional outcome" such as taking on a new job or a new course of studies. These pursuits and accomplishments may not always make you happier. One reason is that increased independence and responsibility often results in greater stress. Likewise, increased family contact can yield more social support as well as more tension. In addition, subjective satisfaction tends to be based on comparisons to a reference group (such as one's peers or community) rather than on actual objective functioning (Li et al., 1998). Satisfaction is based on a comparison of what can be attained; but how do people learn what they can expect to attain? Steven Pinker provides some insight:

A good source of information is what other people have attained. If they can get it, perhaps so can you. Through the ages, observers of the human condition have pointed out the tragedy: people are happy when they feel better off than their neighbors, unhappy when they feel worse off. (1997, p. 390)

For individuals with schizophrenia who are isolated, there may be little awareness of what can be attained. But with increasing community contacts and activities, patients who were previously isolated might become more aware of how much their level of functioning differs from that of healthy members of the community. Conflicting forces act on the satisfaction. On the one hand, objective improvement in functioning should increase satisfaction. On the other, increased awareness of where patients stand compared to people without schizophrenia can decrease satisfaction. The upshot is that all bets are off: Subjective satisfaction in schizophrenia is determined by too many factors. This area of outcome supports Yogi Berra's contention that it is hard to make predictions, especially about the future.

Safety and Welfare

Another outcome domain that is critically important, but only rarely considered as a form of illness outcome, is safety and welfare of the individual (Rosenblatt & Attkisson, 1993), or the interaction between the patient and the community. Problems such as self-injurious behavior (including suicide), drug and alcohol abuse, HIV transmission, violence directed at the patient, and violence committed by the patient are associated with schizophrenia, but not always considered as a form of outcome.

An especially sobering aspect of schizophrenia is its association with suicide, a fact quickly grasped by family members. Although there are dramatic examples of psychotic symptoms leading to suicide (such as hearing voices commanding patients to kill themselves), suicide in schizophrenia is more frequently associated with clinical depression (Saarinen, Lehtonen, & Lonnqvist, 1999). In this excerpt, a mother of a patient describes her painful need for vigilance to safeguard against a suicide attempt by her son:

Our son's first suicide attempt took place while he was in the group home. I had started playing Scrabble with him after his first hospitalization. We both loved the game. It did wonders for his self-esteem to beat his mother, and I am convinced it helped him regain some of his cognitive functioning. He won consistently except when he was decompensating. If I began to win, I knew he was due for a relapse. One evening we played Scrabble, then he went downstairs, swallowed a handful of pills, and waited to die. When nothing happened, he went to the hospital hoping to talk to somebody. The pills hit him while he was waiting to be seen. He narrowly missed dying that evening, but I was not informed until he phoned me himself several days later. I went on an 18-year suicide watch after that, and I slept with my clothes on for the next 10 years. (Malloy, 1998, p. 496)

The bottom line is that schizophrenia carries with it both obvious and hidden costs. It is easy to understand that a relapse and a hospitalization are disruptive and demoralizing. It is less obvious that drug use and self-injurious behavior are, indirectly, manifestations of schizophrenia. In chapter 1, we discussed the extensive disability associated with schizophrenia; it is among the top five causes of disability for young adults in developed countries. This ranking, however, does not include suicide (which contributes to the disability of depression instead). Hence the very high estimates of schizophrenia's disability may actually be underestimates.

Personal Determinants of Functional Outcome

To have any chance of reducing the disability of schizophrenia, we first need to know the determinants of good versus poor functional outcome. Many patients exhibit reduced functioning (including social isolation, interpersonal awkwardness) in the premorbid period before the onset of clinical symptoms. Premorbid functioning tells us something about what we can expect from later functional outcome. After all, it is easier for individuals with schizophrenia to re-learn social and vocational skills that they once knew than it is to learn the skills from scratch. But this begs a chicken and egg question: What were the determinants of functioning before onset of illness? They are probably the same as the determinants of functional outcome after onset of clinical symptoms.

In the previous sections, we have seen that good clinical outcome (including control of psychotic symptoms) does not necessarily lead to good functional outcome. If symptoms are not related to functional outcome, then what is? Of course, many determinants of functional outcome lie entirely outside the individual and are well beyond a clinician's control: Vocational outcome is influenced by local unemployment rates, and availability of case management and social skills programs are influenced by public mental health funding priorities. Several key factors for functional outcome exist within the individual and may be modifiable, including those discussed in the following sections. By identifying these personal determinants of functional outcome, we may start to figure out ways to reduce, even slightly, the disability of the illness.

Neurocognition

Although the neurocognitive deficits of schizophrenia have been recognized for a long time, their functional consequences have only recently been appreciated. Previously, scientists focused somewhat narrowly on attempts to define and characterize the neurocognitive deficits of schizophrenia, such as those described in chapter 4. There were a few earlier findings suggesting that higher intelligence was linked to better functioning in schizophrenia (Heaton & Pendleton, 1981), but these studies attracted less attention than they deserved. Beginning in the early 1990s, several laboratories, including our own, started asking "So what?" What difference does it make that patients have these neurocognitive deficits? The questions have now shifted to understanding the toll these deficits take in the patients' daily lives. Do neurocognitive deficits make it difficult to catch the right bus, prepare a meal, or keep a job? Do they make it hard for patients to maintain communication with their family, or to remember to take their medication?

In general, neurocognitive deficits show highly consistent relationships to functional outcome (Green, 1996; Green, Kern, Braff, & Mintz, 2000). In figure 7.2, neurocognitive areas are shown on the left, and functional outcome areas are shown on the right. The neurocognitive areas (executive functions, types of memory, and vigilance) were all described in chapter 4. Functional outcome areas are grouped into three general categories. The first area, community and daily activities, includes broader aspects of community outcome such as social and vocational outcome, as well as competence in activities of daily living (managing money, shopping for necessities, grooming and hygiene). The second category, social problem-solving skills, is necessary for successful functioning in the community. These skills are usually measured in a laboratory. For example, a person might be shown videotaped vignettes of interpersonal situations (e.g., a husband and wife arguing over which TV show to watch; a customer discussing a billing mistake with a sales clerk). After viewing the vignette, participants are rated on their ability to identify the problem, generate possible solutions to the problem, and then role-play these solutions. The third area is acquisition of skills in social skills training programs. As mentioned in the previous chapter, psychosocial skills programs are designed to teach patients what is needed for successful transition into the community.

One way to assess whether relationships exist between neurocognitive deficits and functional outcome is to count up the number of times studies from different laboratories find the same relationships. Such replications of findings are depicted in figure 7.2, with heavy arrows indicating many replications (at least 4 different studies with the same result), and thin arrows showing fewer replications (2 or 3 studies with the same result). Counting replications in this manner is not the most rigorous way to draw conclusions in science, but the presence of these associations are confirmed when sophisticated statistical analyses are used. The figure shows the replications for separate types of neurocognitive measures (i.e., vigilance, immediate memory,

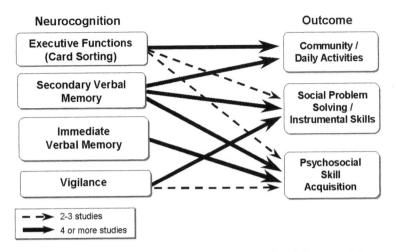

Figure 7.2 ■ *Relationships between neurocognitive deficits and functional outcome. Thfs figure depicts the relationships between neurocognitive deficits and functional outcome areas. Selected neurocognitive constructs are shown on the left, and outcome domains are shown on the right. The arrows indicate findings that were replicated across laboratories, with the heavy arrows reflecting more replications. From Green et al., 2000.*

etc.). Instead of looking at measures individually, an alternative approach is to group several neurocognitive measures together so they form a general neurocognitive summary score. Such general factors usually relate very strongly to outcome, even more strongly than individual measures do (Green et al., 2000).

Some neurocognitive measures appear to be particularly related to outcome. For example, memory for lists of words and written passages (called secondary or episodic memory) has a particularly strong relationship to functional outcome. These relationships with verbal memory are said to have "face validity," meaning that they make sense to a bright 6th grader. To be successful with social skills training programs, it makes sense that participants need to retain material presented by trainers and through videotapes. Beyond the training programs, verbal encoding and retention are needed for success with activities of daily living (such as those for hygiene, transportation, communication, meal preparation, etc) that form the building blocks for adequate functioning in the community.

Conditions other than schizophrenia also involve neurocognitive deficits (including many developmental and neurological disorders). Do neurocognitive deficits account for functional outcome in other conditions as well? Indeed, neurocognitive deficits take a toll on functioning in multiple sclerosis, AIDS, and even in a nonclinical elderly sample (Heaton et al., 1994; Moritz, Kasl, & Berkman, 1995; Rao, Leo, Ellington, & Nauertz, 1991; Van Gorp, Baerwald, Ferrando, McElhiney, & Rabkin, 1999). The upshot is that abilities such as memory and vigilance help us to manuever through our world, and this is as true for schizophrenic patients as it is for elderly retirees. Studies of schizophrenia have probably tapped into universal associations that seem obvious in retrospect, but they were only demonstrated within the past decade.

In contrast to neurocognitive deficits, psychotic symptoms (hallucinations and delusions) are poor predictors and correlates of functional outcome (Green, 1996). This lack of relationship is consistent with the observation that successful control of symptoms with antipsychotic medications has not lead to dramatic improvement in functional outcome. There are indications that other types of symptoms are associated with functional outcome. Although little is known about disorganized cluster of symptoms (including formal thought disorder), this symptom cluster may be related to outcome (Norman et al., 1999; Racenstein, Penn, Harrow, & Schleser, 1999). Also, a clinical condition related to negative symptoms, the deficit syndrome, may be closely connected to functional outcome.

Negative Symptoms and the Deficit Syndrome

As described in the first chapter, negative symptoms include a flattening of emotion (called blunted affect), reduction in speech and movement, and reduced willingness to participate in work, school, and recreational activities. When included in studies of functional outcome, negative symptoms show some relationships, but they typically are not quite as strong as those between neurocognitive deficits and functional outcome (Harvey et al., 1998; Velligan et al., 1997). It is not obvious why the relationships between negative symptoms and functional outcome are not stronger; after all, reduced participation in activities is both a negative symptom and a sign of functional impairment as described in this statement: "I doubt that anyone ever completely recovers from mental illness. I tried to go back to school, but I found that I just could not concentrate and I did not feel motivated" (Hummingbird, 1999, p. 864).

One reason why the relationships are not stronger may be because there are several different causes for negative symptoms. Suppose that someone with schizophrenia withdraws and stops participating in his or her group activities. Such behavior could be the direct result of negative symptoms, but it could also be the result of depression or a recurrence of a delusion that he or she will be hurt when leaving the house. Similarly, if a person appears slowed down, this could be a negative symptom or a medication side effect. How does one separate "true" negative symptoms from all of these imposters? William Carpenter and his colleagues have suggested that true negative symptoms are part of a "deficit syndrome" that is characterized by strong stability over time (Carpenter, Heinrichs, & Wagman, 1988). This stable deficit syndrome, more than negative symptoms in general, is related to functional outcomes such as employment and social functioning (Fenton & McGlashan, 1994). Hence the deficit syndrome, or "true" negative symptoms, constitute another determinant of functional outcome, along with neurocognitive deficits. This may not be entirely surprising because patients with the deficit syndrome tend to have more neurocognitive deficits than those without (Buchanan, Strauss, et al., 1994).

Other Determinants of Outcome: Social Cognition and Insight

Imagine you were unable to recognize the emotions expressed in faces or voices. What would family interactions and work encounters be like? Would you nod at the wrong time, laugh at an inopportune moment, or approach someone who is sending you messages to stay away? Would you inadvertently make other people uncomfortable? Or would you play it safe and start to withdraw? The content of a spoken message is sometimes sufficient to convey the emotion behind it. Most of the time, however, sentences are emotionally ambiguous, and it is the context—the facial expression or the voice quality—that gets the emotional point across. As described in chapter 4, schizophrenic patients show deficits in aspects of social cognition, including identifying emotions from faces and voices.

Social cognition resides in the gray zone between nonsocial neurocognition (such as vigilance and memory) and personal interactions. Because it resides in this interface and has features of both components, social cognition is closely associated with the daily lives of patients. For example, problems in recognizing facial emotions are associated with reduced social competence and social interest for patients on a unit (Mueser et al., 1996; Penn et al., 1996). In our laboratory, Kimmy Kee and colleagues found that the ability to identify emotions in faces and voices is directly related to how well a patient functions in the community one year later, both in terms of work and independent living. Social cognition may be one example of what patients need to re-enter the community and navigate through their world—essentially the "right stuff" for functional outcome (Green & Nuechterlein, 1999b).

Insight, or awareness of illness, may be another example of the right stuff. As the sixth century Chinese philosopher Lao-Tzu observed: "He who knows others is clever; He who knows himself has discernment." Whereas social cognition is awareness of others, insight is awareness of self. Frequently, schizophrenic patients do not know that they have an illness, do not know the purpose of their medications, and are unaware that their symptoms are caused by an illness. Insight in schizophrenia refers to an awareness of symptoms, the consequences of one's illness, and a need for treatment (Amador, Strauss, Yale, & Gorman, 1991; David, Buchanan, Reed, & Almeida, 1992). Degree of insight is related to various outcomes, including hospitalization, social relationships, work, and ability to benefit from psychosocial rehabilitation (Lysaker, Bell, Milstein, Bryson, & Beam-Goulet,

1994; McGlashan & Carpenter, 1981; Schwartz, 1998). Patients with insight are more likely to take their medication and to stay in treatment programs, which reduces the likelihood of rehospitalizations that disrupt community stays. Although many patients have extremely limited insight, it may be modifiable with interventions. Awareness of illness can be taught through educational programs, and more accurate attributions of symptoms can sometimes be conveyed through cognitive behavioral therapy.

From Neurons to Disability

At this time, we can piece together a new view of schizophrenia that has been steadily revealed through careful scientific research over the past decade. It is a view that is based on three pillars of schizophrenia: disrupted neural connections, neurocognitive deficits, and functional impairment. The problems start with subtle failures in communication among groups of neurons and culminate in functional impairment and disability. The question remains as to how each step leads to the other.

The disrupted neural connections stem from early neurodevelopment and can be influenced by prenatal events as varied as influenza, starvation, Rh compatibility, or psychological stress of the mother. Because influenza and psychological stress during pregnancy are far more common than schizophrenia, it means that only a fraction of the individuals exposed to such events develop schizophrenia. Some individuals are more vulnerable to prenatal events than others, and this vulnerability is based largely on genetics. Although it is exceedingly unlikely that schizophrenia will be traced to a single gene, there is little doubt that the disorder has strong genetic contributions and that variants of certain genes (i.e. alleles) can increase or decrease vulnerability to schizophrenia. The search for such genes is a major preoccupation, but despite impressive developments in molecular genetics, research in this area still has a long way to go.

As a result of the events during the early development of the nervous system, neurons can wind up in slightly the wrong place, at slightly the wrong orientation, or with slightly the wrong neurochemical functioning. Problems in neural connections are the consequence. What are the implications of disrupted neural connections? Imagine a symphony orchestra in which the musicians all have slight timing problems; they sometimes come in a little before the beat, and sometimes a little after. The orchestra still makes music, and the timing problems might not be noticeable during slow movements. But these minor problems in timing and coherence will be very noticeable during faster parts where timing is particularly critical. Similarly, neurons that lack optimal connections lose their coherence, and it is especially noticeable when intricate timing is required.

The breakdown of the neural connections is reflected in the neurocognitive deficits of the illness, including problems in attention, memory, perception, sensory gating, and executive functions. These problems start before the onset of symptoms, are present after the symptoms have remitted, and are often found in unaffected first-degree relatives. We are just beginning to understand the neural bases of neurocognitive deficits through the use of structural and functional neuroimaging techniques. These neurocognitive deficits might also serve as alternative phenotypes for studies of molecular genetics, thereby greatly improving the power of these studies to detect illness-related genes. Neurocognitive deficits are key determinants of functional outcome. Other determinants may include the deficit syndrome, social cognition, and insight.

If schizophrenia has a signature, it is functional impairment. Impaired functioning is necessary for a diagnosis, and adequate functioning is necessary for successful community re-entry. Such is the plight of individuals with schizophrenia; the diagnosis carries with it the certainty that patients will need extra effort and assistance to function in the community. Community re-entry skills range from taking public transportation to preparing meals, grooming, and maintaining conversations in the workplace. When one has spent years struggling with schizophrenia, there is no such thing as an easy interpersonal task. Contact with family members needs to be reinstated, and connections with friends rebuilt. Simple communication skills and activities of daily living are difficult to attain, especially if the skills were marginal before the onset of illness.

Nonetheless, there should be no mistake about it—this is a time of optimism for schizophrenia. The first reason for optimism is that we are starting to understand the fundamentals of the illness. With few exceptions, it has been many years since spirits, witches, or "schizophrenogenic" mothers were held responsible for schizophrenia. For the most part, family members no longer feel blamed; they feel confused. The considerably more enlightened explanations, that schizophrenia is a brain disease of hallucinations and delusions, are still perplexing to most people. Schizophrenia has been rendered mysterious at its core. In the words of Kraepelin, the causes of schizophrenia have been wrapped in "impenetrable darkness," and there has been little argument about his conclusion for one hundred years. But we no longer have any reason to retain the overpowering mystery of schizophrenia: It is simply unnecessary baggage at this time. This burdensome illness has its roots in genetic vulnerability and neurodevelopmental processes. Fundamentally, schizophrenia is an illness of disrupted neural connections, and these problems in connections lead to neurocognitive deficits. The neurocognitive deficits, among other factors, lead to functional impairment and its striking disability. In addition, the illness has characteristic symptoms (psychotic, negative, and disorganized) during the active phase that are the focus of treatment. Although the scope of the explanation is sweeping, ranging from neurons to social interactions, there is nothing particularly mysterious about this formulation.

The second reason for optimism is that the treatments are getting better. Discussions about this point tend to revolve around the impressive advances in antipsychotic medications. Indeed, the new generation of antipsychotic medications provide clear advantages compared to earlier medications, including fewer side effects. At the same time, other innovative treatments are popping up like wildflowers. Novel types of pharmacological interventions are being tested that specifically target neurocognitive deficits and negative symptoms, which are critical aspects of the illness that do not normalize with current treatments. In addition, psychosocial interventions (e.g., social skills training, vocational rehabilitation) are becoming more systematized and more available. These nonpharmacological interventions target the activities of daily living, the skills necessary for re-entry into the community, and the interpersonal tasks that are deceptively easy for healthy people and exceedingly difficult for patients. A disorder as complex as schizophrenia is unlikely to respond to one type of treatment. Instead, sights should be set on developing a judicious combination of treatments that will manage symptoms, improve neurocognition, and reduce the disability of schizophrenia. Optimism and schizophrenia are rarely mentioned in the same breath. Nonetheless, an impressive amount of light has recently been shed on the world's most enigmatic disorder, and better days lie ahead.

References

Akbarian, S., Bunney, W. E., Potkin, S. G., Wigal, S. B., Hagman, J. O., Sandman, C. A., & Jones, E. G. (1993). Altered distribution of nicotinamide-adenine dinucleotide phosphate-diaphorase cells in frontal lobe of schizophrenics implies disturbances of cortical development. *Archives of General Psychiatry, 50,* 169–177.

Akbarian, S., Kim, J. J., Potkin, S. G., Hetrick, W. P., Bunney, W. E., & Jones, E. G. (1996). Maldistribution of interstitial neurons in prefrontal white matter of the brains of schizophrenic patients. *Archives of General Psychiatry, 53,* 425–436.

Amador, X. F., Strauss, D. H., Yale, S. A., & Gorman, J. M. (1991). Awareness of illness in schizophrenia. *Schizophrenia Bulletin, 17,* 113–132.

American Psychiatric Association. (1987). *DSM-III-R: Diagnostic and statistical manual of mental disorders* (3rd ed., rev. ed.). Washington, DC: Author.

American Psychiatric Association. (1994). *Diagnostic and statistical manual of mental disorders* (4th ed.). Washington, DC: Author.

Andreasen, N. C., Arndt, S., Swayze II, V., Cizadlo, T., Flaum, M., O'Leary, D., Ehrhardt, J. C., & Yuh, W. T. C. (1994). Thalamic abnormalities in schizophrenia visualized through magnetic resonance image averaging. *Science, 266,* 294–398.

Andreasen, N. C., Nopoulus, P., O'Leary, D. S., Miller, D. D., Wassink, T., & Flaum, M. (1999). Defining the phenotype of schizophrenia: Cognitive dysmetria and its neural mechanism. *Biological Psychiatry, 46,* 908–920.

Andreasen, N. C., Paradiso, S., & O'Leary, D. S. (1998). "Cognitive Dysmetria" as an integrative theory of schizophrenia: A dysfunction in cortical-subcortical-cerebellar circuitry? *Schizophrenia Bulletin, 24,* 203–218.

Andreasen, N. C., Rezai, K., Alliger, R., Swayze, V. W., Flaum, M., Kirchner, P., Cohen, G., & O'Leary, D. S. (1992). Hypofrontality in neuroleptic-naïve patients and in patients with chronic schizophrenia. *Archives of General Psychiatry, 49,* 943–958.

Arnold, S. E., Hyman, B. T., Van Hoesen, G. W., & Damasio, A. R. (1991). Some cytoarchitectural abnormalities of the entorhinal cortex in schizophrenia. *Archives of General Psychiatry, 48,* 625–632.

Barr, C. E., Mednick, S. A., & Munck-Jorgenson, P. (1990). Maternal influenza and schizophrenic births. *Archives of General Psychiatry, 47,* 869–874.

Beck, A T., Rush, A. J., Shaw, B. F., & Emery, G. (1979). *Cognitive therapy of depression.* New York: Guilford.

Benedict, R. H. B., Harris, A. E., Markow, T., McCormick, J. A., Nuechterlein, K. H., & Asarnow, R. F. (1994). Effects of attention training on information processing in schizophrenia. *Schizophrenia Bulletin, 20*(3), 537–546.

Berman, K. F., Zec, R. F., & Weinberger, D. R. (1986). Physiologic dysfunction of dorsolateral prefrontal cortex in schizophrenia. *Archives of General Psychiatry, 43,* 126–135.

Bertolino, A., Esposito, G., Callicott, J. H., Mattay, V. S., Van Horn, J. D., Frank, J. A., Berman K. F., & Weinberger, D. R. (2000). Specific relationship between prefrontal neuronal N-acetyl aspartate and activation of the working memory cortical network in schizophrenia. *American Journal of Psychiatry, 157,* 26–33.

Bertolino, A., Nawroz, S., Mattay, V. S., Barnett, A. S., Duyn, J. H., Moonen, C. T. W., Frank, J. A., Tedeschi, G., & Weinberger, D. R. (1996). Regionally specific pattern of neurochemical pathology in schizophrenia as assessed by multislice proton magnetic resonance spectroscopic imaging. *American Journal of Psychiatry, 153,* 1554–1563.

Bilder, R. M. (1992). Structure-function relations in schizophrenia: Brain morphology and neuropsychology. *Progress in Experimental Personality and Psychopathology Research, 15,* 183–251.

Bleuler, E. (1950). *Dementia praecox or the group of schizophrenias.* New York: International Universities Press.

Bouchard, T. J., Lykken, D. T., McGue, M., Segal, N. L., & Tellegen, A. (1990). Sources of human psychological differences: The Minnesota study of twins reared apart. *Science, 250,* 223–228.

Bracha, H. S., Torrey, E. F., Bigelow, L. B., Lohr, J. B., & Linington, B. B. (1991). Subtle signs of prenatal maldevelopment of the hand ectoderm in schizophrenia: A preliminary monozygotic twin study. *Biological Psychiatry, 30,* 719–725.

Bracha, H. S., Torrey, E. F., Gottesman, I. I., Bigelow, L. B., & Cunniff, C. (1992). Second-trimester markers of fetal size in schizophrenia: A study of monozygotic twins. *American Journal of Psychiatry, 149,* 1355–1361.

Braff, D., Stone, C., Callaway, E., Geyer, M., Glick, I., & Bali, L. (1978). Prestimulus effects on human startle reflex in normals and schizophrenics. *Psychophysiology, 15,* 339–343.

Braff, D. L. (1981). Impaired speed of information processing in nonmedicated schizotypal patients. *Schizophrenia Bulletin, 7*, 499–508.

Braff, D. L., & Saccuzzo, D. P. (1982). Effect of antipsychotic medication on speed of information processing in schizophrenic patients. *American Journal of Psychiatry, 139*, 1127–1130.

Braff, D. L., Saccuzzo, D. P., & Geyer, M. A. (1991). Information processing dysfunctions in schizophrenia: Studies of visual backward masking, sensorimotor gating, and habituation. In S. R. Steinhauer, J. H. Gruzelier, & J. Zubin (Eds.), *Handbook of schizophrenia: Neuropsychology, psychophysiology, and information processing* (Vol. 5, pp. 303–334). Amsterdam: Elsevier.

Braslow, J. (1997). *Mental ills and bodily cures: Psychiatric treatment in the first half of the twentieth century.* Berkeley, CA: University of California Press.

Breitmeyer, B. G. (1984). *Visual masking: An integrative approach.* New York: Oxford University Press.

Brekke, J. S., Levin, S., Wolkon, G., Sobel, E., & Slade, E. (1993). Psychosocial functioning and subjective experience in schizophrenia. *Schizophrenia Bulletin, 19*, 599–608.

Brodoff, A. S. (1998). First person account: Schizophrenia through a sister's eyes: The burden of invisible baggage. *Schizophrenia Bulletin, 14*, 113–116.

Brown, A. S., van Os, J., Driessens, C., Hoek, H. W., & Susser, E. S. (2000). Further evidence of relation between prenatal famine and major affective disorder. *American Journal of Psychiatry, 157*, 190–195.

Buchanan, R. W., Holstein, C., & Breier, A. (1994). The comparative efficacy and long-term effect of clopazine treatment on neuropsychological test performance. *Biological Psychiatry, 36*, 717–725.

Buchanan, R. W., Strauss, M. E., Kirkpatrick, B., Holstein, C., Breier, A., & Carpenter, W. T. (1994). Neuropsychological impairments in deficit vs. nondeficit forms of schizophrenia. *Archives of General Psychiatry, 51*, 804–811.

Buchsbaum, M. S., Haier, R. J., Potkin, S. G., Nuechterlein, K., Bracha, H. S., Katz, M., Lohr, J., Wu, J., Lottenberg, S., Jerabek, P. A., Trenary, M., Tafalla, R., Reynolds, C., & Bunney, W. E. (1992). Frontostriatal disorder of cerebral metabolism in never-medicated schizophrenics. *Archives of General Psychiatry, 49*, 935–942.

Buchsbaum, M. S., Someya, T., Ying Teng, C., Abel, L., Chin, S., Najafi, A., Haier, R. J., Wu, J., & Bunney, W. E. (1996). PET and MRI of the thalamus in never-medicated patients with schizophrenia. *American Journal of Psychiatry, 153*(2), 191–199.

Burmeister, M. (1999). Basic concepts in the study of diseases with complex genetics. *Biological Psychiatry, 45*, 522–532.

Cadenhead, K. S., Perry, W., & Braff, D. L. (1996). The relationship of information-processing deficits and clinical symptoms in schizotypal personality disorder. *Biological Psychiatry, 40*, 853–858.

Caldwell, A. E. (1970). *Origins of psychopharmacology: From CPZ to LSD.* Springfield, IL: Charles C. Thomas.

Cannon, T. D., Mednick, S. A., & Parnas, J. (1989). Genetic and perinatal determinants of structural brain deficits in schizophrenia. *Archives of General Psychiatry, 46,* 883–889.

Carlson, N. R. (1998). *Physiology of behavior* (6th ed.). Needham Heights, MA: Allyn & Bacon.

Carpenter, W. T., Heinrichs, D. W., & Wagman, A. M. I. (1988). Deficit and nondeficit forms of schizophrenia: The concept. *American Journal of Psychiatry, 145,* 578–583.

Cassens, G., Inglis, A. K., Appelbaum, P. S., & Gutheil, T. G. (1990). Neuroleptics: Effects on neuropsychological function in chronic schizophrenic patients. *Schizophrenia Bulletin, 16*(3), 477–499.

Chatterjee, A., Chakos, M., Koreen, A., Geisler, S., Sheitman, B., Woerner, M., Kane, J. M., Alvir, J., & Lieberman, J. A. (1995). Prevalence and clinical correlates of extrapyramidal signs and spontaneous dyskinesia in never-medicated schizophrenic patients. *American Journal of Psychiatry, 152*(12), 1724–1729.

Cherry, S. R., & Phelps, M. E. (1996). Imaging brain function with positron emission tomography. In A. W. Toga & J. C. Mazziotta (Eds.), *Brain mapping: The methods* (pp. 191–221). San Diego: Academic Press.

Ciompi, L. (1980). Catamnestic long-term study on the course of life and aging of schizophrenics. *Schizophrenia Bulletin, 6,* 606–618.

Clementz, B. A., Blumenfeld, L. D., & Cobb, S. (1997). The gamma band response may account for poor P50 suppression in schizophrenia. *NeuroReport, 8,* 3889–3893.

Cohen, J. D., & Servan-Schreiber, D. (1992). Context, cortex, and dopamine: A connectionist approach to behavior and biology in schizophrenia. *Psychological Review, 99,* 45–77.

Cohen, M. S., & Bookheimer, S. Y. (1994). Localization of brain function using magnetic resonance imaging. *Trends in Neurosciences, 17,* 268–277.

Conrad, A. J., Abebe, T., Austin, R., Forsythe, S., & Scheibel, A. (1991). Hippocampal pyramidal cell disarray in schizophrenia as a bilateral phenomenon. *Archives of General Psychiatry, 48,* 413–417.

Cook, J. A., & Razzano, L. (2000). Vocational rehabilitation for persons with schizophrenia: Recent research and implications for practice. *Schizophrenia Bulletin, 26,* 87–103.

Cornblatt, B., Lenzenweger, M. F., Dworkin, R., & Erlenmeyer-Kimling, L. (1992). Childhood attentional dysfunction predicts social deficits in unaffected adults at risk for schizophrenia. *British Journal of Psychiatry, 161*(Suppl. 18), 59–64.

Cornblatt, B., Obuchowski, M., Schnur, D. B., & O'Brien, J. D. (1997). Attention and clinical symptoms in schizophrenia. *Psychiatric Quarterly, 68,* 343–359.

Cornblatt, B. A., & Erlenmeyer-Kimling, L. (1985). Global attentional deviance as a marker of risk for schizophrenia: Specificity and predictive validity. *Journal of Abnormal Psychology, 94,* 470–486.

Csernansky, J. G., Joshi, S., Wang, L., Haller, J. W., Gado, M., Miller, J. P., Grenander, U., & Miller, M. I. (1998). Hippocampal morphometry in schizophrenia by high dimensional brain mapping. *Neurobiology, 95,* 11406–11411.

David, A. S. (1994). Dysmodularity: A neurocognitive model for schizophrenia. *Schizophrenia Bulletin, 20,* 249–255.

David, A. S., Buchanan, A., Reed, A., & Almeida, O. (1992). The assessment of insight in psychosis. *British Journal of Psychiatry, 161,* 599–602.

David, A. S., Malmberg, A., Brandt, L., Allebeck, P., & Lewis, G. (1997). IQ and risk for schizophrenia: A population-based cohort study. *Psychological Medicine, 27,* 1311–1323.

Davidson, M., & Keefe, R. S. E. (1995). Cognitive impairment as a target for pharmacological treatment in schizophrenia. *Schizophrenia Research, 17,* 123–129.

Davidson, M., Reichenberg, A., Rabinowitz, J., Weiser, M., Kaplan, Z., & Mark, M. (1999). Behavioral and intellectual markers for schizophrenia in apparently healthy male adolescents. *American Journal of Psychiatry, 156,* 1328–1335.

Davies, D. R., & Parasuraman, R. (1982). *The psychology of vigilance.* London: Academic Press.

Davis, J. O., & Bracha, H. S. (1996). Prenatal growth marker in schizophrenia: A monozygotic co-twin control study. *American Journal of Psychiatry, 153,* 1166–1172.

Davis, K. L., & Powchik, P. (1995). Tacrine. *Lancet, 345,* 625–630.

Dawson, M. E., Hazlett, E. A., Filion, D. L., Nuechterlein, K. H., & Schell, A. M. (1993). Attention and schizophrenia: Impaired modulation of the startle reflex. *Journal of Abnormal Psychology, 102,* 633–641.

Degreef, G., Ashtari, M., Bogerts, B., Bilder, R. M., Jody, D. N., Alvir, J. M. J., & Lieberman, J. A. (1992). Volumes of ventricular system subdivisions measures from magnetic resonance images in first episode schizophrenic patients. *Archives of General Psychiatry, 49,* 531–537.

DeLisi, L. E., Sakuma, M., Tew, W., Kushner, M., Hoff, A. L., & Grimson, R. (1997). Schizophrenia as a chronic active brain process: A study of progressive brain structural change subsequent to the onset of schizophrenia. *Psychiatry Research, 74,* 129–140.

Deutsch, G. (1992). The nonspecificity of frontal dysfunction in disease and altered states: Cortical blood flow evidence. *Neuropsychiatry, Neuropsychology, and Behavioral Neurology, 5*(4), 301–307.

Dixon, L., Adams, C., & Luckstead, A. (2000). Update on family psychoeducation for schizophrenia. *Schizophrenia Bulletin, 26,* 5–20.

Dohrewend, B. P., Levav, I., Shrout, P. E., Schwartz, S., Naveh, G., Link, B. G., Skodol, A. E., & Stueve, A. (1992). Socioeconomic status and psychiatric disorders: The causation-selection issue. *Science, 255,* 946–951.

Drachman, D. A., & Leavitt, J. (1974). Human memory and the cholinergic system. *Archives of Neurology, 30,* 113–121.

Dykstra, T. (1997). First person account: How I cope. *Schizophrenia Bulletin, 23,* 697–699.

Earle-Boyer, E. A., Serper, M. R., Davidson, M., & Harvey, P. D. (1991). Continuous performance tests in schizophrenic patients: Stimulus and medication effects on performance. *Psychiatry Research, 37,* 47–56.

Fenton, W. S., & McGlashan, T. H. (1994). Antecedents, symptom progression, and long-term outcome of the deficit syndrome in schizophrenia. *American Journal of Psychiatry, 151,* 351–356.

Flashman, L. A., Flaum, M., Gupta, S., & Andreasen, N. C. (1996). Soft signs and neuropsychological performance in schizophrenia. *American Journal of Psychiatry, 153,* 526–532.

Freedman, R., Adler, L. E., Gerhardt, G. A., Waldo, M., Baker, N., Rose, G. M., Drebing, C., Nagamoto, H., Bickford-Winer, P., & Franks, R. (1987). Neurobiological studies of sensory gating in schizophrenia. *Schizophrenia Bulletin, 13,* 669–678.

Freedman, R., Adler, L. E., & Leonard, S. (1999). Alternative phenotypes for the complex genetics of schizophrenia. *Biological Psychiatry, 45,* 551–558.

Freedman, R., Coon, H., Myles-Worsley, M., Orr-Urtreger, A., Olincy, A., Davis, A., Polymeropoulos, M., Holik, J., Hopkins, J., Hoff, M., Rosenthal, J., Waldo, M. C., Reimherr, F., Wender, P., Yaw, J., Young, D. A., Breese, C. R., Adams, C., Patterson, D., Adler, L. E., Kruglyak, L., Leonard, S., & Byerley, W. (1997). Linkage of a neurophysiological deficit in schizophrenia to a chromosome 15 locus. *Proceedings of the National Academy of Sciences of the United States of America, 94,* 587–592.

Frith, C. D. (1992). *The cognitive neuropsychology of schizophrenia.* Hove, U.K.: Lawrence Erlbaum Associates.

Fulton, J. F. (1928). Observations upon the vascularity of the human occipital lobe during visual activity. *Brain, 51,* 310–320.

Fuster, J. M. (1989). *The prefrontal cortex: Anatomy, physiology, and neuropsychology of the frontal lobe* (2nd ed.). New York: Raven Press.

Garety, P. A., Fowler, D., & Kuipers, E. (2000). Cognitive-behavioral therapy for medication-resistant symptoms. *Schizophrenia Bulletin, 26,* 73–86.

Glantz, L. A., & Lewis, D. A. (1997). Reduction of synaptophysin immunoreactivity in the prefrontal cortex of subjects with schizophrenia: Regional and diagnostic specificity. *Archives of General Psychiatry, 54,* 943–952.

Goff, D. C., Tsai, G., Manoach, D. S., & Coyle, J. T. (1995). Dose-finding trial for D-cycloserine added to neuroleptics for negative symptoms in schizophrenia. *American Journal of Psychiatry, 152,* 1213–1215.

Gold, J. M., Randolph, C., Carpenter, C. J., Goldberg, T. E., & Weinberger, D. R. (1992). Forms of memory failure in schizophrenia. *Journal of Abnormal Psychology, 101,* 487–494.

Goldberg, T. E., Ragland, J. D., Torrey, E. F., Gold, J. M., Bigelow, L. B., & Weinberger, D. R. (1990). Neuropsychological assessment of monozygotic twins discordant for schizophrenia. *Archives of General Psychiatry, 47,* 1066–1072.

Goldman-Rakic, P. S. (1993). Working memory and the mind. In *Mind and brain: Readings from Scientific American magazine* (pp. 67–77). New York: W. H. Freeman & Co.

Gottesman, I. I. (1991). *Schizophrenia genesis: The origins of madness.* New York: W. H. Freeman & Co.

Gottesman, I. I., & Shields, J. (1982). *Schizophrenia: The epigenetic puzzle.* Cambridge, U.K.: Cambridge University Press.

Green, M. F. (1993). Cognitive remediation in schizophrenia: Is it time yet? *American Journal of Psychiatry, 150*(2), 178–187.

Green, M. F. (1996). What are the functional consequences of neurocognitive deficits in schizophrenia? *American Journal of Psychiatry, 153*(3), 321–330.

Green, M. F. (1998). *Schizophrenia from a neurocognitive perspective: Probing the impenetrable darkness.* Boston: Allyn & Bacon.

Green, M. F., Bracha, S. H., Satz, P., & Christenson, C. (1994). Preliminary evidence for an association between minor physical anomalies and second trimester neurodevelopment in schizophrenia. *Psychiatry Research, 53*, 119–127.

Green, M. F., Kern, R. S., Braff, D. L., & Mintz, J. (2000). Neurocognitive deficits and functional outcome in schizophrenia: Are we measuring the "right stuff"? *Schizophrenia Bulletin, 26*, 119–136.

Green, M. F., Marshall, B. D., Wirshing, W. C., Ames, D., Marder, S. R., McGurk, S., Kern, R. S., & Mintz, J. (1997). Does risperidone improve verbal working memory in treatment-resistant schizophrenia? *American Journal of Psychiatry, 154*, 799–804.

Green, M. F., & Nuechterlein, K. H. (1999a). Cortical oscillations and schizophrenia: Timing is of the essence. *Archives of General Psychiatry, 56*, 1007–1008.

Green, M. F., & Nuechterlein, K. H. (1999b). Should schizophrenia be treated as a neurocognitive disorder? *Schizophrenia Bulletin, 25*, 309–319.

Green, M. F., Nuechterlein, K. H., & Breitmeyer, B. (1997). Backward masking performance in unaffected siblings of schizophrenia patients: Evidence for a vulnerability indicator. *Archives of General Psychiatry, 54*, 465–472.

Green, M. F., Nuechterlein, K. H., Breitmeyer, B., & Mintz, J. (1999). Backward masking in unmedicated schizophrenic patients in psychotic remission: Possible reflections of aberrant cortical oscillations. *American Journal of Psychiatry, 156*, 1367–1373.

Green, M. F., Nuechterlein, K. H., & Mintz, J. (1994). Backward masking in schizophrenia and mania: Specifying a mechanism. *Archives of General Psychiatry, 51*, 939–944.

Green, M. F., Satz, P., & Christenson, C. (1994). Minor physical anomalies in schizophrenia patients, bipolar patients, and their siblings. *Schizophrenia Bulletin, 20*, 433–440.

Green, M. F., Satz, P., Gaier, D. J., Ganzell, S., & Kharabi, F. (1989). Minor physical anomalies in schizophrenia. *Schizophrenia Bulletin, 15*, 91–99.

Green, M. F., Satz, P., Ganzell, S., & Vaclav, J. F. (1992). Wisconsin card sorting test performance in schizophrenia: Remediation of a stubborn deficit. *American Journal of Psychiatry, 149*, 62–67.

Green, M. F., Satz, P., Smith, C., & Nelson, L. (1989). Is there atypical handedness in schizophrenia? *Journal of Abnormal Psychology, 98*, 57–61.

Green, M. F., & Walker, E. (1986). Symptom correlates of vulnerability to backward masking in schizophrenia. *American Journal of Psychiatry, 143*, 181–186.

Greenblat, L. (2000). First person account: Understanding health as a continuum. *Schizophrenia Bulletin, 26*, 243–245.

Gur, R. E., Cowell, P., Turetsky, B. I., Gallacher, F., Cannon, T., Bilker, W., & Gur, R. C. (1998). A follow-up magnetic resonance imaging study of schizophrenia: Relationship of neuroanatomical changes to clinical and neurobehavioral measures. *Archives of General Psychiatry, 55*, 145–152.

Gur, R. E., & Pearlson, G. D. (1993). Neuroimaging in schizophrenia research. *Schizophrenia Bulletin, 19*(2), 337–353.

Guy, J. D., Majorski, L. V., Wallace, C. J., & Guy, M. P. (1983). The incidence of minor physical anomalies in adult male schizophrenics. *Schizophrenia Bulletin, 9*, 571–582.

Hagger, C., Buckley, P., Kenny, J. T., Friedman, L., Ubogy, D., & Meltzer, H. Y. (1993). Improvement in cognitive functions and psychiatric symptoms in treatment-refractory schizophrenic patients receiving clozapine. *Biological Psychiatry, 34*, 702–712.

Harding, C. M. (1988). Course types in schizophrenia: An analysis of European and American studies. *Schizophrenia Bulletin, 14*, 633–643.

Harding, C. M., Brooks, G. W., Ashikaga, T., Strauss, J. S., & Breier, A. (1987). The Vermont longitudinal study: II. Long-term outcome for subjects who retrospectively met *DSM-III* criteria for schizophrenia. *American Journal of Psychiatry, 144*, 727–735.

Harvey, P. D., Howanitz, E., Parrella, M., White, L., Davidson, M., Mohs, R. C., Hoblyn, J., & Davis, K. L. (1998). Symptoms, cognitive functioning, and adaptive skills in geriatric patients with lifelong schizophrenia: A comparison across treatment sites. *American Journal of Psychiatry, 155*, 1080–1086.

Harvey, P. D., Keefe, R. S. E., Mitroupolou, V., & DuPre, R. (1996). Information-processing markers of vulnerability to schizophrenia: Performance of patients with schizotypal and nonschizotypal personality disorders. *Psychiatry Research, 60*, 49–56.

Harvey, P. D., Parrella, M., White, L., Mohs, R. C., & Davis, K. L. (1999). Convergence of cognitive and functional decline in poor outcome schizophrenia. *Schizophrenia Research, 35*, 77–84.

Hazlett, E. A., Buchsbaum, M. S., Haznedar, M. M., Singer, M. B., Schnur, D. B., Jimenez, E. A., Buchsbaum, B. R., & Troyer, B. T. (1998). Prefrontal cortex glucose metabolism and startle eyeblink modification abnormalities in unmedicated schizophrenia patients. *Psychophysiology, 35*, 186–198.

Heaton, R. K. (1981). *Wisconsin card sorting test manual.* Odessa, FL: Psychological Assessment Resources.

Heaton, R. K., & Pendleton, M. G. (1981). Use of neuropsychological tests to predict adult patients' everyday functioning. *Journal of Consulting and Clinical Psychology, 49*, 807–821.

Heaton, R. K., Velin, R. V., McCutchan, A., Gulevich, S. J., Atkinson, J. H., Wallace, M. R., Godfrey, H. P. D., Kirson, D. A., & Grant I. (1994). Neuropsychological impairment in human immunodeficiency virus-infection: Implications for employment. *Psychosomatic Medicine, 56,* 8–17.

Hegarty, J. D., Baldessarini, R. J., Tohen, M., Waternaux, C., & Oepen, G. (1994). One hundred years of schizophrenia: A meta-analysis of the outcome literature. *American Journal of Psychiatry, 151,* 1409–1416.

Heinrichs, R. W., & Zakzanis, K. K. (1998). Neurocognitive deficit in schizophrenia: A quantitative review of the evidence. *Neuropsychology, 12,* 426–445.

Heinssen, R. K., Liberman, R. P., & Kopelowicz, A. (2000). Psychosocial skills training for schizophrenia: Lessons from the laboratory. *Schizophrenia Bulletin, 26,* 21–46.

Helgason, L. (1990). Twenty years' follow-up of first psychiatric presentation for schizophrenia: What could have been prevented? *Acta Psychiatrica Scandinavica, 81,* 231–235.

Hemsley, D. R. (1987). An experimental psychological model for schizophrenia. In H. Hafner, W. F. Gattaz, & A. Janzarik (Eds.), *Search for the causes of schizophrenia* (pp. 179–188). Heidelberg, Germany: Springer-Verlag.

Hemsley, D. R. (1994). Perceptual and cognitive abnormalities as the bases for schizophrenic symptoms. In D. S. Anthony & J. C. Cutting (Eds.), *The neuropsychology of schizophrenia* (pp. 97–116). Hove, U.K.: Lawrence Erlbaum Associates.

Heston, L. L. (1966). Psychiatric disorders in foster home reared children of schizophrenic mothers. *British Journal of Psychiatry, 112,* 819–825.

Hoenig, J. (1995). Schizophrenia: Clinical section. In G. E. Berrios & R. Porter (Eds.), *A history of clinical psychiatry* (pp. 336–348). New York: New York University Press.

Hoff, A. L., Faustman, W. O., Wieneke, M., Espinoza, S., Costa, M., Wolkowitz, O., & Csernansky, J. G. (1996). The effects of clozapine on symptom reduction, neurocognitive function, and clinical management in treatment refractory state hospital schizophrenic inpatients. *Neuropsychopharmacology, 15*(4), 361–369.

Hoffman, R. E., & McGlashan, T. H. (1993). Parallel distributed processing and the emergence of schizophrenic symptoms. *Schizophrenia Bulletin, 19,* 119–140.

Hollister, J. M., Laing, P., & Mednick, S. A. (1996). Rhesus incompatibility as a risk factor for schizophrenia in male adults. *Archives of General Psychiatry, 53,* 19–24.

Holzman, P. S., & Matthysse, S. (1990). The genetics of schizophrenia: A review. *Psychological Science, 1*(5), 279–286.

Hummingbird. (1999). First person account: Schizophrenia, substance abuse, and HIV. *Schizophrenia Bulletin, 25,* 863–866.

Huttunen, M. O., & Niskanen, P. (1978). Prenatal loss of father and psychiatric disorders. *Archives of General Psychiatry, 35,* 429–431.

Hyman, S. E. (1999). Introduction to the complex genetics of mental disorders. *Biological Psychiatry, 45,* 518–521.

Ismail, B., Cantor-Graae, E., & McNeil, T. F. (1998). Neurological abnormalities in schizophrenic patients and their siblings. *American Journal of Psychiatry, 155,* 84–89.

Izard, C. E. (1971). *The face of emotion.* New York: Appleton-Century-Crofts.

Jakob, H., & Beckman, H. (1986). Prenatal developmental disturbances in the limbic allocortex in schizophrenics. *Journal of Neural Transmission, 65,* 303–326.

Johnstone, E. C., Crow, T. J., Frith, C. D., Stevens, J., & Kreel, L. (1976). Cerebral ventricular size and cognitive impairment in chronic schizophrenia. *Lancet, I,* 924–926.

Kahneman, D. (1973). *Attention and effort.* Englewood Cliffs, NJ: Prentice-Hall.

Kane, J. M. (1996). Schizophrenia. *The New England Journal of Medicine, 334*(1), 34–41.

Kapur, S., Zipursky, R., Jones, C., Remington, G., & Houle, S. (2000). Relationship between dopamine D_2 occupancy, clinical response, and side effects: A double-blind PET study of first-episode schizophrenia. *American Journal of Psychiatry, 157,* 514–520.

Kapur, S., Zipursky, R., Jones, C., Shammi, C. S., Remington, G., & Seeman, P. (2000). A positron emission tomography study of quetiapine in schizophrenia: A preliminary finding of an antipsychotic effect with only transiently high dopamine D_2 receptor occupancy. *Archives of General Psychiatry, 57,* 553–559.

Keefe, R. S. E., Silva, S. G., Perkins, D. O., & Lieberman, J. A. (1999). The effects of atypical antipsychotic drugs on neurocognitive impairment in schizophrenia: A review and meta-analysis. *Schizophrenia Bulletin, 25,* 201–222.

Kendler, K. S., & Diehl, S. R. (1993). The genetics of schizophrenia: A current, genetic-epidemiologic perspective. *Schizophrenia Bulletin, 19*(2), 261–285.

Kern, R. S., Green, M. F., Marshall, B. D., Wirshing, W. C., Wirshing, D., McGurk, S., Marder, S., & Mintz, J. (1999). Risperidone vs. haloperidol on secondary memory: Can newer antipsychotic medications aid learning? *Schizophrenia Bulletin, 25,* 223–232.

Kern, R. S., Wallace, C. J., Hellman, S. G., Womack, L. M., & Green, M. F. (1996). A training procedure for remediating WCST deficits in chronic psychotic patients: An adaptation of errorless learning principles. *Journal of Psychiatric Research, 30,* 283–294.

Kety, S. S., Wender, P. H., Jacobsen, B., Ingraham, L. J., Jansson, L., Faber, B., & Kinney, D. K. (1994). Mental illness in the biological and adoptive relatives of schizophrenic adoptees: Replication of the Copenhagen study in the rest of Denmark. *Archives of General Psychiatry, 51,* 442–455.

Kety, S. S., Woodford, R. B., Harmel, M. H., Freyhan, F. A., Appel, K. E., & Schmidt, C. F. (1948). Cerebral blood flow and metabolism in schizophrenia: The effects of barbiturate semi-narcosis, insulin coma, and electroshock. *American Journal of Psychiatry, 104,* 765–770.

Knight, R., Elliot, D. S., & Freedman, E. G. (1985). Short-term visual memory in schizophrenics. *Journal of Abnormal Psychology, 94,* 427–442.

Kovelman, J. A., & Scheibel, A. B. (1984). A neurohistological correlate of schizophrenia. *Biological Psychiatry, 19,* 1602–1621.

Kraepelin, E. (1971). *Dementia praecox and paraphrenia.* Huntington, NY: Robert E. Krieger Publishing.

Krystal, J. H., Karper, L. P., Seibyl, J. P., Freeman, G. K., Delaney, R., Bremner, J. D., Heninger, G. R., Bowers, M. B., & Charney, D. S. (1994). Subanesthetic effects of the noncompetitive NMDA antagonist, ketamine, in humans; psychotomimetic, perceptual, cognitive, and neuroendocrine responses. *Archives of General Psychiatry, 51,* 199–214.

Kwon, J. S., O'Donnell, B. F., Wallenstein, G. V., Greene, R. W., Hirayasu, Y., Nestor, P. G., Hasselmo, M. E., Potts, F., Shenton, M. E., & McCarley, R. W. (1999). Gamma frequency-range abnormalities to auditory stimulation in schizophrenia. *Archives of General Psychiatry, 56,* 1001–1006.

Lam, C. W., & Berrios, G. E., (1992). Psychological concepts and psychiatric symptomatology in ancient Chinese medical texts. *History of Psychiatry, 3,* 117–128.

Latz, A., & Kornetsky, C. (1965). The effects of chlorpromazine and secobarbital under two conditions of reinforcement on the performance of chronic schizophrenic subjects. *Psychopharmacologia, 7,* 77–88.

Leff, J., Kuipers, L., Berkowitz, R., & Sturgeon, D. (1985). A controlled trial of social intervention in the families of schizophrenic patients: Two-year follow-up. *British Journal of Psychiatry, 146,* 594–600.

Lehman, A. F. (2000). Commentary: What happens to psychosocial treatment on the way to the clinic? *Schizophrenia Bulletin, 26,* 137–139.

Levitan, C., Ward, P. B., & Catts, S. V. (1999). Superior temporal gyral volumes and laterality correlates of auditory hallucinations in schizophrenia. *Biological Psychiatry, 46,* 955–962.

Li, L., Young, D., Wei, H., Zhang, Y., Zheng, Y., Xiao, S., Wang, X., & Chen, X. (1998). The relationship between objective life status and subjective life satisfaction with quality of life. *Behavioral Medicine, 23,* 149–159.

Liddle, P. F., Friston, K. J., Frith, C. D., Hirsch, S. R., Jones, T., & Frackowiak, R. S. J. (1992). Patterns of cerebral blood flow in schizophrenia. *British Journal of Psychiatry, 160,* 179–186.

Lim, K. O., Hedehus, M., Moseley, M., de Crespigny, A., Sullivan, E. V., & Pfefferbaum, A. (1999). Compromised white matter tract integrity in schizophrenia inferred from diffusion tensor imaging. *Archives of General Psychiatry, 56,* 367–374.

Lim, K. O., Tew, W., Kushner, M., Chow, K., Matsumoto, B., & DeLisi, L. E. (1996). Cortical gray matter volume deficit in patients with first-episode schizophrenia. *American Journal of Psychiatry, 153,* 1548–1553.

Lysaker, P., Bell, M., Milstein, R., Bryson, G., & Beam-Goulet, J. (1994). Insight and psychosocial treatment compliance in schizophrenia. *Psychiatry, 57,* 307–315.

McCarley, R. W., Wible, C. G., Frumin, M., Hirayasu, Y., Levitt, J. J., Fischer, I. A., & Shenton, M. E. (1999). MRI anatomy of schizophrenia. *Biological Psychiatry, 45,* 1099–1119.

McGhie, A., & Chapman, J. (1961). Disorders of attention and perception in early schizophrenia. *British Journal of Medical Psychology, 34,* 103–116.

McGlashan, T. H. (1988). A selective review of the recent North American long-term follow-up studies of schizophrenia. *Schizophrenia Bulletin, 14,* 515–542.

McGlashan, T. H., & Carpenter, W. T. (1981). Does attitude toward psychosis relate to outcome? *American Journal of Psychiatry, 138,* 797–801.

McGlashan, T. H., & Hoffman, R. E. (2000). Schizophrenia as a disorder of developmentally reduced synaptic connectivity. *Archives of General Psychiatry, 57,* 637–648.

McGue, M., Gottesman, I. I., & Rao, D. C. (1983). The transmission of schizophrenia under a multifactorial threshold model. *American Journal of Human Genetics, 35,* 1161–1178.

McGuffin, P., Asherson, P., Owen, M., & Farmer, A. (1994). The strength of the genetic effect: Is there room for an environmental influence in the aetiology of schizophrenia? *British Journal of Psychiatry, 164,* 593–599.

Machon, R., Mednick, S., & Huttunen, M. (1997). Adult major affective disorder after prenatal exposure to an influenza epidemic. *Archives of General Psychiatry, 54,* 322–328.

McNeil, T., Cantor-Graae, E., & Weinberger, D. R. (2000). Relationship of obstetric complications and differences in brain structures in monozygotic twin pairs discordant for schizophrenia. *American Journal of Psychiatry, 157,* 203–212.

Malhotra, A. K., Pinals, D. A., Weingartner, H., Sirocco, K., Missar, C. D., Pickar, D., & Breier, A. (1996). NMDA receptor function and human cognition: The effects of ketamine in healthy volunteers. *Neuropsychopharmacology, 14,* 301–307.

Malhotra, A. K., Inam, A. S., & Chopra, H. D. (1981). Do psychiatric patients reject themselves? *Indian Journal of Psychiatry, 23,* 44–48.

Malloy, R. (1998). First person account: My voyage through turbulence. *Schizophrenia Bulletin, 24,* 495–497.

Mann, S. B. (1999). First person account: Talking through medication issues: One family's experience. *Schizophrenia Bulletin, 25,* 407–409.

Marder, S. R., Davis, J. M., & Chouinard, G. (1997). The effects of risperidone on the five dimensions of schizophrenia derived by factor analyses: Combined results of the North American trials. *Journal of Clinical Psychiatry, 58,* 538–546.

Marengo, J. T., Harrow, M., Lannin-Kettering, I. B., & Wilson, A. (1985). The assessment of bizarre-idiosyncratic thinking: A manual for scoring responses to verbal tests. In M. Harrow & D. Quinlan (Eds.), *Disordered thinking and schizophrenic psychopathology* (pp. 394–449). New York: Gardner Press.

Markow, T. A., & Gottesman, I. I. (1989). Fluctuating dermatoglyphic asymmetry in psychotic twins. *Psychiatry Research, 29,* 37–43.

Medalia, A., Aluma, M., Tryon, W., & Merriam, A. (1998). Effectiveness of attention training in schizophrenia. *Schizophrenia Bulletin, 24,* 147–152.

Mednick, S. A., Machon, R. A., Huttunen, M. O., & Bonett, D. (1988). Adult schizophrenia following prenatal exposure to an influenza epidemic. *Archives of General Psychiatry, 45,* 189–192.

Mednick, S. A., Parnas, J., & Schulsinger, F. (1987). The Copenhagen high-risk project, 1962–86. *Schizophrenia Bulletin, 13*(3), 485–495.

Mellor, C. S. (1992). Dermatoglyphic evidence of fluctuating asymmetry in schizophrenia. *British Journal of Psychiatry, 160,* 467–472.

Meltzer, H. Y., & McGurk, S. R. (1999). The effect of clozapine, risperidone, and olanzapine on cognitive function in schizophrenia. *Schizophrenia Bulletin, 25,* 233–255.

Miller, S., Saccuzzo, D., & Braff, D. (1979). Information processing deficits in remitted schizophrenics. *Journal of Abnormal Psychology, 88,* 446–449.

Mirsky, A. F., Ingraham, L. J., & Kugelmass, S. (1995). Neuropsychological assessment of attention and its pathology in the Israeli cohort. *Schizophrenia Bulletin, 21*(2), 193–204.

Moller, H.-J., & Von Zerssen, D. (1995). Course and outcome of schizophrenia. In S. R. Hirsch & D. R. Weinberger (Eds.), *Schizophrenia* (pp. 106–127). Oxford, U.K.: Blackwell Science.

Moore, M. T., Nathan, D., Elliott, A. R., & Laubach, C. (1935). Encephalographic studies in mental disease. *American Journal of Psychiatry, 92*(1), 43–67.

Moritz, D. J., Kasl, S. V., & Berkman, L. F. (1995). Cognitive functioning and the incidence of limitations in activities of daily living in an elderly community sample. *American Journal of Epidemiology, 142,* 41–49.

Mueser, K. T., Bond, G. R., Drake, R. E., & Resnick, S. G. (1998). Models of community care for severe mental illness: A review of research on case management. *Schizophrenia Bulletin, 24,* 37–74.

Mueser, K. T., Doonan, B., Penn, D. L., Blanchard, J. J., Bellack, A. S., Nishith, P., & DeLeon, J. (1996). Emotion recognition and social competence in chronic schizophrenia. *Journal of Abnormal Psychology, 105,* 271–275.

Murphy, M. A. (1997). First person account: Meaning of psychosis. *Schizophrenia Bulletin, 23,* 541–543.

Murray, C. J. L., & Lopez, A. D. (Eds.). (1996). *The global burden of disease.* Boston: Harvard School of Public Health.

Murray, R. M., & Jones, P. (1995). Back to the future in schizophrenia research. In J. Hafner & W. F. Gattaz (Eds.), *Search for the causes of schizophrenia* (Vol. 3, pp. 186–192). Berlin: Springer-Verlag.

Murray, R. M., Jones, P., O'Callaghan, E., Takei, N., & Sham, P. (1992). Genes, viruses, and neurodevelopmental schizophrenia. *Journal of Psychiatric Research, 26,* 225–235.

Nasar, S. (1998). *A beautiful mind.* New York: Simon & Schuster.

Norman, R. M. G., Malla, A. K., Cortese, L., Cheng, S., Diaz, K., McIntosh, E., McLean, T. S., Rickwood, A., & Voruganti, L. P. (1999). Symptoms and cognition as predictors of community functioning: A prospective analysis. *American Journal of Psychiatry, 156,* 400–405.

Nuechterlein, K. H. (1983). Signal detection in vigilance tasks and behavioral attributes among offspring of schizophrenic mothers and among hyperactive children. *Journal of Abnormal Psychology, 92,* 4–28.

Nuechterlein, K. H. (1991). Vigilance in schizophrenia and related disorders. In S. R. Steinhauer, J. H. Gruzelier, & J. Zubin (Eds.), *Handbook of schizophrenia* (Vol. 5, pp. 397–433). Amsterdam: Elsevier.

Nuechterlein, K. H., & Dawson, M. E. (1984a). A heuristic vulnerability/stress model of schizophrenic episodes. *Schizophrenia Bulletin, 10*(2), 300–312.

Nuechterlein, K. H., & Dawson, M. E. (1984b). Information processing and attentional functioning in the developmental course of schizophrenia disorders. *Schizophrenia Bulletin, 10,* 160–203.

Nuechterlein, K. H., Dawson, M. E., & Green, M. F. (1994). Information-processing abnormalities as neuropsychological vulnerability indicators for schizophrenia. *Acta Psychiatrica Scandinavica, 90*(Suppl. 384), 71–79.

O'Callaghan, E., Larkin, C., Kinsella, A., & Waddington, J. L. (1991). Familial, obstetric, and other clinical correlates of minor physical anomalies in schizophrenia. *American Journal of Psychiatry, 148,* 479–483.

O'Callaghan, E., Sham, P., Takei, N., Glover, G., & Murray, R. M. (1991). Schizophrenia after prenatal exposure to 1957 A2 influenza epidemic. *Lancet, 337,* 1248–1250.

Oldendorf, W. H. (1980). *The quest for an image of the brain: Computerized tomography in the perspective of past and future imaging methods.* New York: Raven Press.

O'Leary, D. S., Andreasen, N. C., Hurtig, R. R., Kesler, M. L., Rogers, M., Arndt, S., Cizadlo, T., Watkins, L., Boles Ponto, L. L., Kirchner, P. T., & Hichwa, R. D. (1996). Auditory attentional deficits in patients with schizophrenia. *Archives of General Psychiatry, 53,* 633–641.

Olney, J. W., & Farber, N. B. (1995). Glutamate receptor dysfunction and schizophrenia. *Archives of General Psychiatry, 52,* 998–1007.

Orzack, M. H., Kornetsky, C., & Freeman, H. (1967). The effects of daily administration of carphenazine on attention in the schizophrenic patient. *Psychopharmacologia, 11,* 31–38.

Palmer, B. W., Heaton, R. K., Paulsen, J. S., Kuck, J., Braff, D., Harris, M. J., Zisook, S., & Jeste, D. V. (1997). Is it possible to be schizophrenic yet neuropsychologically normal? *Neuropsychology, 11,* 437–446.

Paul, G. L., & Lentz, R. J. (1977). *Psychological treatment of chronic mental patients.* Cambridge, MA: Boston University Press.

Penn, D. L., Corrigan, P. W., Bentall, R. P., Racenstein, J. M., & Newman, L. (1997). Social cognition in schizophrenia. *Psychological Bulletin, 121,* 114–132.

Penn, D. L., & Mueser, K. T. (1996). Research update on the psychosocial treatment of schizophrenia. *American Journal of Psychiatry, 153,* 607–617.

Penn, D. L., Spaulding, W. D., Reed, D., & Sullivan, M. (1996). The relationship of social cognition toward behavior in chronic schizophrenia. *Schizophrenia Research, 20,* 327–335.

Pinker, S. (1997). *How the mind works.* New York: Norton.

Porter, R. (1995). Epilepsy: Social section. In G. E. Berrios & R. Porter (Eds.), *A history of clinical psychiatry* (pp. 164–173). New York: New York University Press.

Pulver, A. E. (2000). Search for schizophrenia susceptibility genes. *Biological Psychiatry, 47,* 221–230.

Purdon, S. E., Jones, B. D. W., Stip, E., Labelle, A., Addington, D., David, S. R., Breier, A., & Tollefson, G. D. (2000). Neuropsychological change in early phase schizophrenia during 12 months of treatment with olanzapine, risperidone, and haloperidol. *Archives of General Psychiatry, 57,* 249–258.

Racenstein, J. M., Penn, D., Harrow, M., & Schleser, R. (1999). Thought disorder and psychosocial functioning in schizophrenia: The concurrent and predictive relationships. *Journal of Nervous and Mental Disease, 187,* 281–289.

Rao, S. M., Leo, G. J., Ellington, L., & Nauertz, T. (1991). Cognitive dysfunction in multiple sclerosis: II. Impact on employment and social functioning. *Neurology, 41,* 692–696.

Rapoport, J. L., Giedd, J. N., Blumenthal, J., Hamburger, S., Jeffries, N., Fernandez, T., Nicolson, R., Bedwell, J., Lenane, M., Zijdenbos, A., Paus, T., & Evans, A. (1999). Progressive cortical change during adolescence in childhood-onset schizophrenia: A longitudinal magnetic resonance imaging study. *Archives of General Psychiatry, 56,* 649–654.

Raz, S., & Raz, N. (1990). Structural brain abnormalities in the major psychoses: A quantitative review of the evidence from computerized imaging. *Psychological Bulletin, 108* (1), 93–108.

Rosenblatt, A., & Attkisson, C. C. (1993). Assessing outcomes for sufferers of severe mental disorder: A conceptual framework and review. *Evaluation and Program Planning, 16,* 347–363.

Rosenthal, D., Wender, P. H., Kety, S. S., Welner, J., & Schulsinger, F. (1971). The adopted-away offspring of schizophrenics. *American Journal of Psychiatry, 128,* 307–311.

Rund, B. R. (1993). Backward-masking performance in chronic and nonchronic schizophrenics, effectively disturbed patients, and normal control subjects. *Journal of Abnormal Psychology, 102,* 74–81.

Saarinen, P. I., Lehtonen, J., & Lonnquvist, J. (1999). Suicide risk in schizophrenia: An analysis of 17 consecutive suicides. *Schizophrenia Bulletin, 25,* 533–542.

Salibi, N., & Brown, M. A. (1998). *Clinical MR spectroscopy: First principles.* New York: Wiley-Liss.

Satz, P., & Green, M. F. (1999). Atypical handedness in schizophrenia: Some methodological and theoretical issues. *Schizophrenia Bulletin, 25,* 63–78.

Saykin, A. J., Gur, R. C., Gur, R. E., Mozley, P. D., Mozley, L. H., Resnick, S. M., Kester, D. B., & Stafiniak, P. (1991). Neuropsychological function in schizophrenia: Selective impairment in memory and learning. *Archives of General Psychiatry, 48,* 618–624.

Schwartz, B. D., Winstead, D. K., & Adinoff, B. (1983). Temporal integration deficit in visual information processing by chronic schizophrenics. *Biological Psychiatry, 18,* 1311–1320.

Schwartz, R. C. (1998). The relationship between insight, illness, and treatment outcome in schizophrenia. *Psychiatric Quarterly, 69,* 1–22.

Selemon, L. D., Rajkowska, G., & Goldman-Rakic, P. S. (1995). Abnormally high neuronal density in the schizophrenic cortex. *Archives of General Psychiatry, 52,* 805–818.

Servan-Schreiber, D., Cohen, J. D., & Steingard, S. (1996). Schizophrenic deficits in the schizophrenia. *Archives of General Psychiatry, 53,* 1105–1112.

Shakow, D. (1946). The nature of deterioration in schizophrenic conditions. *Nervous and Mental Disease Monographs, 70.*

Shenton, M. E., Kinkinis, R., Jolesz, F. A., Pollack, S. D., LeMay, M., Wible, C. G., Hokama, H., Martin, J., Medcalf, D., Coleman, M., & McCarley, R. W. (1992). Left-lateralized temporal lobe abnormalities in schizophrenia and their relationship to thought disorder: A computerized, quantitative MRI study. *New England Journal of Medicine, 327,* 604–612.

Silbersweig, D. A., Stern, E., Frith, C., Cahill, C., Holmes, A., Grootonk, S., Seaward, J., McKenna, P., Chua, S. E., Schnorr, L., Jones, T., & Frackowiak, R. S. J. (1995). A functional neuroanatomy of hallucinations in schizophrenia. *Nature, 378,* 176–179.

Spaulding, W. D., Fleming, S. K., Reed, D., Lam, M., Sullivan, M., & Storzbach, D. (1999). Cognitive functioning in schizophrenia: Implications for psychiatric rehabilitation. *Schizophrenia Bulletin, 25,* 275–289.

Spitzer, R. L., Gibbon, M., Skodol, A. E., Williams, J. B. W., & First, M. B. (1989). *DSM-III-R Casebook.* Washington DC: American Psychiatric Press.

Spohn, H. E., Lacoursiere, R. B., Thompson, K., & Coyne, L. (1977). Phenothiazine effects on psychological and psychophysiological dysfunction in chronic schizophrenics. *Archives of General Psychiatry, 34,* 633–644.

Stein, L. I., & Test, M. A. (1980). Alternatives to mental hospital treatment: I. Conceptual model treatment program and clinical evaluation. *Archives of General Psychiatry, 37,* 392–397.

Stevens, A. A., Goldman-Rakic, P. S., Gore, J. C., Fulbright, R. K., & Wexler, B. E. (1998). Cortical dysfunction in schizophrenia during auditory word and tone working memory demonstrated by functional magnetic resonance imaging. *Archives of General Psychiatry, 55,* 1097–1103.

Sundquist, A. (1999). First person account: Family psychoeducation can change lives. *Schizophrenia Bulletin, 25,* 619–621.

Susser, E., Neugebauer, R., Hoek, H. W., Brown, A. S., Lin, S., Labovitz, D., & Gorman, J. M. (1996). Schizophrenia after prenatal famine. *Archives of General Psychiatry, 53,* 25–31.

Susser, E. S., & Lin, S. P. (1992). Schizophrenia after prenatal exposure to the Dutch Hunger Winter of 1944–1945. *Archives of General Psychiatry, 49,* 983–988.

Sweeney, J. A., Keilp, J. G., Haas, G. L., Hill, J., & Weiden, P. J. (1991). Relationships between medication treatments and neuropsychological test performance in schizophrenia. *Psychiatry Research, 37,* 297–308.

Swerdlow, N. R., Braff, D. L., Taaid, N., & Geyer, M. A. (1994). Assessing the validity of an animal model of deficient sensorimotor gating in schizophrenic patients. *Archives of General Psychiatry, 51,* 139–154.

Swerdlow, N. R., & Koob, G. F. (1987). Dopamine, schizophrenia, mania, and depression: Toward a unified hypothesis of cortico-striato-pallido-thalamic function. *Behavioral and Brain Sciences, 10,* 197–245.

Thomas, M. A. & Alger, J. R. (1997). MR spectroscopy of the brain. In A. DeSalles & R. Lufkin (Eds.), *Minimally invasive therapy of the brain.* New York: Thieme.

Tienari, P. (1991). Interaction between genetic vulnerability and family environment: The Finnish adoptive family study of schizophrenia. *Acta Psychiatrica Scandinavica, 84,* 460–465.

Tsai, G., Yang, P., Chung, L.-C., Lange, N., & Coyle, J. T. (1998). D-serine added to antipsychotics for the treatment of schizophrenia. *Biological Psychiatry, 44,* 1081–1089.

Tsuang, M. T., Stone, W. S., & Faraone, S. V. (2000). Toward reformulating the diagnosis of schizophrenia. *American Journal of Psychiatry, 157,* 1041–1050.

Van Gorp, W. G., Baerwald, J. P., Ferrando, S. J., McElhiney, M. C., & Rabkin, J. G. (1999). The relationship between employment and neuropsychological impairment in HIV infection. *Journal of the International Neuropsychological Society, 6,* 534–539.

Velligan, D. I., Mahurin, R. K., Diamond, P. L., Hazelton, B. C., Eckert, S. L., & Miller, A. L. (1997). The functional significance of symptomatology and cognitive function in schizophrenia. *Schizophrenia Research, 25,* 21–31.

Wagner, P. S. (1996). First person account: A voice from another closet. *Schizophrenia Bulletin, 22*(2), 399–401.

Waldrop, M. F., & Halverson, C. F. (1971). Minor physical anomalies and hyperactive behavior in young children. In J. Hellmuth (Ed.), *Exceptional infant: Studies in abnormalities* (Vol. 2, pp. 343–380). New York: Brunner/Mazel.

Walker, E. F. (1994). Developmentally moderated expressions of the neuropathology underlying schizophrenia. *Schizophrenia Bulletin, 20,* 453–480.

Walker, E. F., & DiForio, D. (1997). Schizophrenia: A neural diathesis-stress model. *Psychological Review, 104,* 667–685.

Walker, E. F., Grimes, K. E., Davis, D. N., & Smith, A. J. (1993). Childhood precursors of schizophrenia: Facial expressions of emotion. *American Journal of Psychiatry, 150,* 1654–1660.

Walker, E. F., Savoie, T., & Davis, D. (1994). Neuromotor precursors of schizophrenia. *Schizophrenia Bulletin, 20,* 441–451.

Weiden, P. J., Scheifler, P. L., Diamond, R. J., & Ross, R. (1999). *Breakthroughs in antipsychotic medications: A guide for consumers, families, and clinicians.* New York: Norton.

Weinberger, D. R. (1987). Implications of normal brain development for the pathogenesis of schizophrenia. *Archives of General Psychiatry, 44,* 660–669.

Weinberger, D. R. (1995). From neuropathology to neurodevelopment. *Lancet, 346,* 552–557.

Weinberger, D. R., Berman, K. F., Suddath, R., & Torrey, F. E. (1992). Evidence of dysfunction of a prefrontal-limbic network in schizophrenia: A magnetic resonance imaging and regional cerebral blood flow study of discordant monozygotic twins. *American Journal of Psychiatry, 149*(7), 890–897.

Weinberger, D. R., Berman, K. F., & Zec, R. F. (1986). Physiologic dysfunction of dorsolateral prefrontal cortex in schizophrenia. *Archives of General Psychiatry, 43,* 114–124.

Weinberger, D. R., & Lipska, B. K. (1995). Cortical maldevelopment, anti-psychotic drugs, and schizophrenia: A search for common ground. *Schizophrenia Research, 16,* 87–110.

Wexler, B. E., Hawkins, K. A., Rounsaville, B., Anderson, M., Sernyak, M. J., & Green, M. F. (1997). Normal neurocognitive performance after extended practice in patients with schizophrenia. *Schizophrenia Research, 26,* 173–180.

Woods, B. T. (1998). Is schizophrenia a progressive neurodevelopmental disorder? Toward a unitary pathogenetic mechanism. *American Journal of Psychiatry, 155,* 1661–1670.

Wyatt, R. J. (1996). Neurodevelopmental abnormalities and schizophrenia: A family affair. *Archives of General Psychiatry, 53,* 11–15.

Wykes, T., Reeder, C., Corner, J., Williams, C., & Everitt, B. (1999). The effects of neurocognitive remediation on executive processing in patients with schizophrenia. *Schizophrenia Bulletin, 25,* 291–307.

Index

Abebe, T., 42
Abel, L., 108
accessory symptoms, 10
    effect on treatment emphasis, 11
N-acetylaspartate
    association with activation in the
        prefrontal cortex induced by
        card sorting tests, 117
    in the brain, magnetic resonance
        spectroscopy studies of, 113–14
acetylcholine
    improvement of memory with
        administration of, 132
    study of possible relationship with
        schizophrenia, 64
acetylcholine receptor, blocking, to
    treat side effects of antipsychotic
    drugs, 127
activation task, for functional
    neuroimaging, 107–10
Adams, C., 68, 78, 141
Addington, D., 133
Adinoff, B., 73
Adler, L. E., 65, 68, 77, 78, 79
adolescence, connection with onset of
    schizophrenia, 48

adoptees
    schizophrenia in children of
        schizophrenic mothers, 58
    of schizophrenic parents, rate of
        schizophrenia in, 59
adoption studies, differentiating
    genetic and environmental factors
    with, 58–60
affective disorders, risks of,
    relationship to influenza or
    starvation, 34
agonist, function of drugs, defined,
    105–6
agranulocytosis, as a side effect of
    clozapine, 128
akathisia, as a side effect of
    antipsychotic drugs, 127
Akbarian, S., 43–44
alcoholism, chronic, hypofrontality in,
    108
Alger, J. R., 113
Allebeck, P., 37
alleles, defined, 60
Alliger, R., 108
allocation, of attentional resources, 91
Almeida, O., 164